JOB ACCESSIBILITY and the EMPLOYMENT and SCHOOL ENROLLMENT of TEENAGERS

Keith R. Ihlanfeldt
Georgia State University

1992

W.E. UPJOHN Institute for Employment Research
Kalamazoo, Michigan

Library of Congress Cataloging-in-Publication Data

Ihlanfeldt, Keith R.
    Job accessibility and the employment and school enrollment of
teenagers / Keith R. Ihlanfeldt.
        p.   cm.
    Includes bibliographical references and index.
    ISBN 0-88099-125-0 — ISBN 0-88099-126-7 (pbk.)
    1. Minority teenagers—Employment—United States.   2. Urban youth—
Employment—United Atates.   3. School attendance—United States.
4. Dropouts—Employment—United States.   I. Title.
HD6273.I44   1992
331.11'423—dc20   92-24549
                                                                                        CIP

ACKNOWLEDGMENTS

I am grateful to the W.E. Upjohn Institute for Employment Research for providing financial support for the research described in this monograph. Financial support was also provided by the Research Program Committee of the College of Business Administration at Georgia State University.

A number of people were very helpful to me in writing this monograph. Harry Holzer, Julie Hotchkiss, Tim Sass, David Sjoquist, and Mary Beth Walker were kind enough to read parts of my draft manuscript and provide me with useful comments. I also benefited from the comments of two anonymous reviewers. Finally, I owe a special debt of gratitude to Tim Bartik, who provided invaluable advice on how to make my draft manuscript more reader-friendly.

Research assistance was provided by Joe Zhu and Adam Chen. Jane Leonard, as she has on so many other occasions, once again provided me with expert computer programming help. Assistance in programming was also provided by Brent Moulton.

The staff of the Policy Research Center at Georgia State University did an excellent job in typing and proofreading this monograph. I especially would like to thank Sharon DePeaza, Vanessa Jamison, Jim Reteneller, and Sharon Weaver for their efforts in helping me to complete this project.

The publications staff of the Upjohn Institute was excellent. I thank Elizabeth Sherman and Judy Gentry for their editing, and Sue McMurray for her work in publicizing the book.

Finally, I thank my wife Susan for her understanding, encouragement, and love.

THE AUTHOR

Keith Ihlanfeldt is Professor of Economics and Senior Research Associate in the Policy Research Center at Georgia State University. Since obtaining his Ph.D. degree from Washington University in 1978, his research has focused on housing economics and urban labor markets. Currently, he is studying poverty among mainland Puerto Ricans and spatial variation in labor market discrimination within metropolitan areas. He has published numerous articles, which have appeared in the *American Economic Review, Economic Inquiry, Southern Economic Journal, Journal of Urban Economics*, and other academic journals.

CONTENTS

1

Introduction

Most social scientists would agree that the high rate of joblessness among black youths is one of this country's worst social problems. This joblessness contributes to the large differences in family income that continue to exist among the races. In addition, the joblessness among black male youths has been hypothesized to be a cause of the high rate of illegal activity (Viscusi 1986) and female-headed families (Wilson 1987) within the black community. Existing evidence, while sparse, lends support to both of these hypotheses. Finally, a number of studies have shown that when black youths are unable to develop on-the-job skills and work attitudes, they experience relatively lower wages and higher unemployment as they grow older (Stevenson 1978; Osterman 1978; Meyer and Wise 1982).

While evidence contrary to this conclusion exists (Ellwood 1982; Becker and Hills 1980), the possibility that black youth unemployment has long-run "scarring effects" reinforces the need to identify the causes of the black youth employment problem. Unfortunately, these causes are not well understood. Factors frequently mentioned as contributors to the problem include discrimination against blacks in the labor market, cultural differences among the races — resulting in a lesser willingness to work among black youths — and the absence of positive role models for youths within inner city black neighborhoods. While these are plausible hypotheses, little evidence exists regarding their relative importance, because generating such evidence requires data that are generally unavailable.

Another attractive hypothesis, more amenable to empirical investigation, is the spatial mismatch hypothesis of John Kain (1968). According to this theory, housing market segregation and the suburbanization of low-skill jobs have acted together to cause blacks to live farther from jobs than whites. Poorer access to jobs is believed to decrease the level of black employment because information on available jobs declines with distance and/or blacks are unwilling or unable to make the longer required commute. The spatial mismatch hypothesis is appealing as an explanation for the black youth employment problem because there is little debate concerning the truth of its premises—housing markets remain highly segregated along racial lines and youth-intensive jobs, such as those found in the service sector, are now concentrated within white suburban areas.[1] Despite these facts, studies by Ellwood (1986) and Leonard (1986b) have yielded no support for the spatial mismatch hypothesis and have therefore concluded, to use Ellwood's now famous aphorism: "Thus the problem isn't space. It's race." In other words, joblessness among black youths is purely a racial phenomenon that has nothing to do with the distance blacks must commute in order to secure employment.

This book has three principal aims. First, I intend to resurrect the spatial mismatch hypothesis as an explanation for the black youth employment problem by providing a considerable amount of evidence that strongly suggests that job access (i.e., distance to jobs) has an important effect on the job probabilities of both black and white youths. These findings, along with additional evidence demonstrating that blacks have decidedly worse access to jobs than whites, implies that the spatial mismatch hypothesis has an important role to play in understanding employment rate differences between the races. A second aim is to empirically demonstrate that job access is also related to the high school dropout problem that has reached crisis proportions within inner cities. Evidence is provided that indicates that poor job access prevents many teenagers from staying in school and working part time. Most frequently, these youths end up out of school without a legitimate job. The final aim of the book is to convince the reader that poor access to jobs, not only is a cause of the joblessness among black youths, but is generally important in explaining the relatively low economic welfare of urban blacks. Here my approach is to critically evaluate each of the 30 studies that has empirically investigated the spatial mismatch hypothesis. My assessment of the literature is contrary to that of Jencks and

Mayer (1990a), who have concluded that the evidence has been so highly mixed that "no prudent policy analyst should rely on it." I argue that if the results from studies that suffer from obvious methodological flaws are put aside, the remaining evidence from studies that are above reproach provides strong and consistent support for the hypothesis. The literature is useful to the formulation and implementation of antipoverty policy.

The research contained in this book builds upon what might be considered a pilot study that was done using 1980 Public-Use Microdata Sample (hereafter referred to as 1980 Public-Use Sample) data for the Philadelphia metropolitan area (U.S. Bureau of Census 1983a, 1983b). In that study, the job probabilities of both black and white youths were found to be strongly affected by the nearness of available jobs. In addition, our estimates suggested that from a third to a half of the employment rate gap between black and white youths can be attributed to differences in job access, depending on the youth group considered. Groups were defined by age, enrollment status, and whether a youth lived at home or on his/her own.

Our work with Philadelphia data, however, raised many more questions than were answered. These questions can be categorized into two groups. The questions in the first group all have a common theme; namely, how general are the strong job access effects observed for white and black Philadelphia youths? For example, are job access effects important for metropolitan areas other than Philadelphia? Hughes (1990) has found that the ghettos of Philadelphia are more isolated from economic opportunity than those located in other metropolitan areas; hence, our Philadelphia results may be unique. Also, do job access differentials explain any of the differences that exist between white and Hispanic youth employment rates? These differentials, while smaller than those existing between whites and blacks, are large enough to be considered a policy concern. Other interesting questions include whether or not the effect of job access on youth employment varies with family income, the size of the metropolitan area, or a youth's residential location—i.e., the central city versus the suburbs—within the metropolitan area.

In the second group of questions raised by our earlier work, there is but a single, although exceedingly important, issue; namely, does an improvement in intraurban job accessibility result in a tradeoff relationship between youth employment and school enrollment? This concern was first expressed by Duncan (1965) more than 25 years ago: "These results suggest, however, that a successful policy to reduce unemployment among drop-outs might well have the side effect of encouraging boys to drop-out of school before high school graduation." While better job access may increase the opportunity cost of staying in school, it also may enable youths desirous of present earnings to work part time while enrolled in school. Without part-time job opportunities located nearby, these youths may drop out either to search for full-time employment or to engage in illicit income-producing activity. Adopting "job access improvement policies" is problematic without knowing how job access impinges upon the school enrollment decisions of individual teenagers.

This book addresses the above questions using expanded samples in comparison to the Philadelphia sample employed in our earlier work. Samples of youths are drawn from the 1980 Public-Use Sample tapes for 50 different metropolitan areas throughout the United States. The same travel-time-based measures of job access employed in our pilot study are used, along with an extensive set of control variables, to explain the probability that a youth is employed and the probability that he/she is enrolled in school. The job access effect on youth employment is found to be remarkably robust across the various groups analyzed in this study and differential job accessibility is found to be important in explaining differences in employment rates among the groups.

The effect of job access on school enrollment is investigated by first developing a utility maximization model that assumes that the employment and enrollment decisions of teenagers are interrelated. This theoretical model yields multinomial logit as the empirical model, which treats the employment and enrollment decisions as jointly endogenous. Better job access is *not* found to increase the probability of dropping out of high school. For younger teenagers, aged 16 to 17 years old, a change in job access is found to have a neutral effect on the school enrollment decision. For older teenagers, aged 18 to 19 years old, a frequent finding is that improved job access results in a lower probability of dropping out of high school. It is of considerable policy interest that this effect is found to be the strongest for black males, a group for whom the drop-out problem has been of particular concern.

The principal policy implication of the research presented in this book is a need for efforts to improve job accessibility for inner city minority youth. In particular, two types of policies are recommended: (1) policies to improve the minority teenager's knowledge of more distant job openings, and (2) policies to reduce the transportation costs these youths incur in commuting to more distant jobs. While some communities have already adopted such policies, the vast majority have not. One of the goals of this book is to prod policymakers at all levels of government to more seriously consider "job access improvement policies" as a way of dealing with the black youth employment problem. A desirable feature of such policies — in contrast to the traditional human capital augmentation programs tried in the past — is that improvements in job access hold the promise of providing handsome paybacks in a relatively short period of time.

The remainder of this introductory chapter provides some documentation of the magnitude of the black youth employment problem and how this problem has evolved over time. In addition, selected studies that have made at least some contribution to our understanding of the problem are cited.

Table 1.1, beginning with the 1950s, gives decade averages of annualized employment rates for black and white teenagers, aged 16 to 19 years old, broken down by race and gender. In the early postwar years, black and white male employment rates were essentially the same; however, the trend since then contrasts sharply between the races. For whites, employment rates have been remarkably stable, with the decade average employment rate for each of the four postwar decades roughly equal to .50. In other words, about half of the white male civilian population of 16 to 19-year-olds has consistently been employed. For blacks, the trend in employment rates has been continuously downward. The decade average was .48 in the 1950s, .40 in the 1960s, .31 in the

1970s, and .28 in the 1980s. The employment rates of black male teenagers have, therefore, fallen both absolutely and relative to those of whites. Today, whites, in comparison to blacks, are almost twice as likely to have a job.[2]

The intertemporal trend in the employment rates of black female teenagers is quite different from that observed for black males. Black female employment rates show no downward trend at all and have remained close to .25 over the entire 40-year time period. The employment rates of white females are higher than those of black females for all four decades; hence, in contrast to the situation observed for males, the postwar period did not begin with black and white females having similar employment rates. For the decade of the 1950s, the white average employment rate was about one-and-one-half times higher than that for blacks. The racial gap in employment rates for females expanded after 1970, as the result of rather dramatic increases in the employment rates of whites. Today, as is true for males, white females are roughly twice as likely to hold a job as black females.[3]

While I could find no studies that have dealt with the employment rate trends of female teenagers, there has been research on black males. Cogan (1982) presents table 1.2, which I have updated by adding

Table 1.1   Decade Average Employment Rates for 16 to 19-Year-Olds by Race and Sex

	Males			Females		
	White	**Black[a]**	**Black/White**	**White**	**Black**	**Black/White**
1950s	.505	.480	.96	.366	.248	.68
1960s	.479	.400	.83	.358	.232	.65
1970s	.535	.312	.58	.444	.223	.50
1980s	.508	.276	.54	.480	.251	.52

SOURCE: U.S. Department of Labor, *Employment and Training Report of the President, 1979* and *Employment and Earnings*, January issues, 1979–1990.

NOTE: The figures are decade averages of the annual employment rate. The annual employment rates were computed for the civilian noninstitutional population of 16 to 19-year-olds.

[a] The figures for blacks include other nonwhites, who represent about 10 percent of the totals.

columns for 1980, to demonstrate that the aggregate trend in the black employment rate masks important differences in region-specific employment patterns.[4] Two conclusions can be drawn from this table. First, as Cogan notes, virtually all of the decline between 1950 and 1970 in the aggregate black teenager employment rate is the result of a sharp decline in the southern employment rate. In fact, the employment rates for the other three regions in 1970 were almost identical to what they were in 1950. Second, between 1970 and 1980, black employment rates declined in every region. These declines were small in the West and South, but were a substantial 5.5 and 6.4 percentage points in the North Central and Northeast regions, respectively.

Cogan provides regression evidence in support of his argument that the decline in the black employment rate in the South between 1950 and 1970 was the result of two factors: (1) the mechanization of agricultural production, which drove blacks from rural areas, where youths were in high demand as farm laborers, to urban areas; and (2) the inability of

Table 1.2   Male Youth Employment-to-Population Ratios by Region: 1950–1980

	Blacks			Whites		
	1950	**1970**	**1980**	**1950**	**1970**	**1980**
United States	46.6	27.0	23.8	40.4	40.5	46.7
Northeast	23.5	26.1	19.6	33.2	39.6	41.9
	(10.9)[a]	(16.2)	(17.6)	(25.4)	(23.5)	(22.0)
North Central	28.1	27.8	22.3	46.7	45.0	47.9
	(11.9)	(19.0)	(19.2)	(29.8)	(29.6)	(28.6)
South	54.8	27.4	25.8	42.5	37.7	45.8
	(71.5)	(53.7)	(54.3)	(31.5)	(29.0)	(31.2)
West	23.3	24.6	23.8	33.8	29.0	47.0
	(5.7)	(11.2)	(8.8)	(13.3)	(17.9)	(18.2)

SOURCE: 1950, 1970: Cogan (1982). 1980: U.S. Bureau of Census (1984). *1980 Census of Population: Detailed Characteristics, U.S. Summary.*

NOTE: The employment data are percentages of the 16 to 19-year-old male population employed, excluding Alaska and Hawaii.

[a] The numbers in parentheses are the percentages of the racial group living in the region.

urban blacks to obtain nonfarm jobs because of the minimum wage, particularly through increases in its coverage in the 1960s. Other factors identified by Margo and Finegan (1991) are the growth in school enrollment of southern blacks and the decline in the labor force participation of those enrolled in school. The combined evidence, therefore, suggests that both demand-side and supply-side changes are important in understanding the time pattern in the employment rates of southern black male youths.

While the work of Cogan and Margo and Finegan helps to resolve part of the black youth employment enigma, there remain the issues of why black male employment rates declined after 1970 in the northern regions and why there exist for both males and females large differences in the employment rates of blacks and whites. No empirically verifiable explanation has been provided for the post-1970 trends. The spatial mismatch hypothesis, however, is appealing as an explanation for the post-1970 regional changes in black employment rates because the rate of job decentralization was more virulent in the North, where employment rates sharply declined, than in the West and South, where only small declines occurred.[5] For example, for the six largest metropolitan areas in the North and East, the percentage of manufacturing jobs located within central cities declined from 55 percent in 1967 to 41 percent in 1982. In contrast, for the six largest metropolitan areas in the South and West, the percentage of manufacturing jobs located within central cities remained almost unchanged—48 percent in 1967 and 45 percent in 1982.[6]

Regarding the existing gap in youth employment rates between whites and blacks, as mentioned above, our Philadelphia study and the results contained in this book support the notion that racial differences in job access play an important role. Other research suggests that other factors may also be relevant. Feldstein and Ellwood (1982) have found that from 21 percent to 33 percent of the difference in nonemployment rates between white and nonwhite out-of-school teenagers can be attributed to differences between the groups in age, family income, and years of schooling. The relative importance of each of these factors was not investigated. In addition, from a policy perspective, the findings of

Feldstein and Ellwood are not very useful, since each of their variables may capture multiple influences. For example, youth from higher income families may have a higher probability of working because they have better access to jobs, a stronger work ethic, or higher levels of job-searching and job-retaining abilities.

Other research that has some bearing on our understanding of the racial gap in youth employment rates is contained in the National Bureau of Economic Research volume on the black youth employment crisis, edited by Freeman and Holzer (1986). The lion's share of this research was based on the Inner-City Black Youth Survey, which consisted of black men, aged 16 to 24, living in poverty areas within the cities of Boston, Chicago, and Philadelphia. As Freeman and Holzer acknowledge, an important weakness of these data is that they cannot be used to compare inner city youths with other youths. Although the research based on the Inner-City Black Youth Survey provided important new information on the factors influencing black youth employment, it is only suggestive of possible factors that may help to explain racial differences in youth employment rates. Other data sources were also employed by the authors contributing to the volume, including the youth cohort of the National Longitudinal Surveys of Labor Market Experience, the 1970 Public Use Sample, and an "audit" project that sent black and white youths out to interview for identical jobs in an attempt to detect discrimination in the labor market.

In their summary of the research contained in the volume, Freeman and Holzer categorize the factors found to affect the labor market outcomes of black youths into those likely to alter the demand for labor and those likely to alter the supply of labor. On the demand side, the major determinants of youth joblessness were found to be (1) the state of the local labor market, (2) the proportion of women in the labor force, (3) the employment status of the youth's family, and (4) the presence of employer discrimination. On the supply side, the evidence suggested that the following factors were important: (1) church attendance, (2) the presence of long-term career goals, (3) the perception of illegal income opportunities, (4) the years of education, and (5) the household situation (i.e., whether the youth lived in a household receiving welfare or residing in public housing). Labor market discrimination against black youths obviously contributes to the racial gap in youth employment rates.[7] To determine whether the other factors listed by Freeman and Holzer help explain this gap, however, additional research that would investigate how these variables impinge on the employment of white youth and how the levels of these variables differ between the races is needed.

The rest of this book is organized into four chapters. Chapter 2 reviews the spatial mismatch literature. Chapter 3 focuses on the first group of questions raised by our earlier work. Estimates are provided of the importance of job access to youth employment for black, white, and Hispanic youths; for youths living in different sized metropolitan areas; for youths living in central city and suburban areas; for youths with different family incomes; and for youths in and out of school. Chapter 4 explores the issue of the effect of job access on school enrollment. And finally, Chapter 5 summarizes the findings presented in chapters 3 and 4 and discusses the public policy implications of these findings.

NOTES

[1] For evidence on the continuance of racial segregation in the housing market, see Kain (1985). He reports that the fraction of black households living outside central cities rose from 18.1 percent in 1970 to 25.8 percent in 1980. However, this had little effect on segregated housing patterns, because most of the increase in the number of black suburban households was the result of the expansion of central city ghettos across central city lines and the growth of suburban concentrations of blacks.

[2] The white and black employment rates for male teenagers were .51 and .28 for the year 1990.

[3] The white and black employment rates for female teenagers were .48 and .27 for the year 1990.

[4] The census data required to compute the regional employment rates for 1990 have not yet been made available by the U.S. Census Bureau.

[5] An alternative explanation for the post-1970 decline in black male youth employment rates in the North is that job opportunities for youths became scarcer, either because of local recessions or the structural transformations of local economies. However, this hypothesis is inconsistent with the employment rates reported for white male youths in table 1.2. In both the Northeast and North Central regions these rates increased, albeit slightly, between 1970 and 1980. These changes are also consistent with job decentralization, since the job accessibility of white youths should improve as the spatial distribution of jobs shifts in favor of the suburbs.

[6] These percentages are reported by Heilbrun (1987, p. 42). His source was the U.S. Bureau of the Census, *Economic Censuses*, various dates.

[7] The conclusion that black youths face discrimination from employers was based on the results obtained from the audit project. While these results suggested that blacks are treated less favorably than whites, the sample was too limited to be used to determine the possible importance of discrimination as an explanation for racial differences in youth employment rates. A more recent audit project conducted by the Urban Institute was based on a larger sample (Turner et al. 1991b). While this study did not attempt to relate discrimination to racial differences in youth employment rates, the results provide strong evidence that young black males encounter significant discrimination in the labor market. Specifically, in 20 percent of the black/white audits, the minority job seeker was treated less favorably by potential employers. Also of considerable interest was the finding that young Hispanic males are more likely than blacks to be treated unfairly. Hispanics were treated less favorably than their white counterparts in 31 percent of the cases.

2

Review and Assessment of the Job Access Literature

This chapter provides a comprehensive review of the studies of which I am aware that have dealt with the relationship between intrametropolitan job accessibility and the economic welfare of urban blacks. Although the empirical work presented in later chapters pertains only to youths, I have two reasons for critiquing all of the literature on job access, not just the small portion that focuses on youth. First, as noted in chapter 1, an aim of this book is to convince the reader that the poor access to jobs possessed by urban blacks is generally important to our understanding of their inferior economic welfare. I believe that the review contained in this chapter will substantiate this point. Second, by demonstrating the general importance that job access has on black economic welfare, the results of this study for youths become more credible. If greater distances to jobs adversely affect black adults, we would certainly expect black youths also to be harmed, since teenagers are more dependent on nearby jobs. Certainly, the policy significance of my findings is enhanced by recognizing that my conclusions are consistent, rather than at odds, with previous studies offering reliable evidence on the accessibility issue.

The literature on intrametropolitan job accessibility originated with John Kain (1968). Over the past 23 years, 30 studies have been published that have explored the issues raised in Kain's seminal article. Many of these studies offer evidence on what is labelled Kain's "spatial mismatch hypothesis." This terminology is problematic, however, since it was never used by Kain and he advanced not one, but rather three distinct hypotheses. The failure to distinguish between Kain's original three hypotheses has been a source of confusion in the empirical literature. This review will attempt to avoid this confusion by relating the evidence provided by each study to a specific hypothesis.

In reviewing any literature as voluminous as the one under consideration, a classification scheme must be adopted. Many alternative classifications might be useful. Studies could be classified chronologically, for example, since there is a clear demarcation between the early studies appearing soon after Kain's article and a group of more recent studies that began appearing in the middle 1980s.[1] Other possible classification schemes include those based upon the methodological approach adopted, the type of data utilized (micro versus aggregate), the dependent variable analyzed (earnings versus employment), the age group considered (youth versus adults) and, of course, the results obtained (pro versus con). Since many of the studies dealing with job access issues have been plagued by numerous methodological problems, the basis of classification used in this review will be by methodological approach. In addition, the few studies that have focused on youths will receive special attention.

The rest of this chapter will be organized as follows. First, Kain's three hypotheses will be discussed and the evidence he provided in support of them evaluated. Second, the various methodological approaches that have been employed to study job access will be critically reviewed. Third, the work that has been done on job accessibility and youth employment will be summarized and evaluated. The chapter will conclude with an overall assessment of the job access literature.

Kain's Hypotheses, Empirical Results, and Early Critics

Kain's three hypotheses can be simply stated: (1) residential segregation affects the geographical distribution of black employment; (2) residential segregation increases black unemployment; and (3) the negative effect of housing segregation on black employment is magnified by the decentralization of jobs. Underlying these hypotheses are a number of premises. The first suggests that black residential segregation within metropolitan areas is not voluntary, but is largely the result of racial discrimination in the housing market. This thesis is supported by considerable empirical evidence.[2] Additional premises propose that commuting is costly to blacks and that information on job opportunities declines with distance. As a result, blacks are more likely to work within or close to their residential neighborhoods, which is Kain's first hypothesis. Another factor identified by Kain that may reinforce this tendency is the possibility that blacks encounter less consumer discrimination in those areas where blacks are a larger percentage of the resident population. White customers may have an aversion to dealing with black employees, which causes employers to hire fewer blacks in predominantly white areas. This hypothesis is sometimes labelled the "sheltered workplace hypothesis" in the post-Kain literature.

The notion behind Kain's second hypothesis is that because discrimination constrains the residential locations of blacks, their job opportunity set is smaller than it would be if their locational choices were dependent on the same forces affecting whites, namely, preferences, prices, and incomes. A smaller job opportunity set results in higher black unemployment because there is a lesser chance that a successful match will occur between worker and job.

Kain's third hypothesis, the negative effect of housing segregation on black employment is magnified by the decentralization of jobs, is what most people have in mind when they make reference to his spatial mismatch hypothesis. There is a spatial mismatch in the sense that jobs are available for which blacks would qualify, but they are either unaware of these opportunities or cannot commute to these jobs because of the distances involved. There is, therefore, a surplus of workers relative to the number of available jobs in those areas where the black population is concentrated, and a shortage of resident labor relative to the number of jobs outside these areas.

The surplus of resident labor within black areas will result in the higher unemployment that Kain hypothesized if wage rates are inflexible in a downward direction. If wages are flexible, however, the labor surplus will be eliminated by wage rates falling to their equilibrium level. It is also possible that some workers who cannot find jobs in or near the ghetto are able to commute to more distant jobs, but they, nevertheless, suffer a welfare loss by earning a lower wage net of commuting costs. Job decentralization combined with involuntary housing segregation, therefore, may reduce the economic welfare of blacks by making it more difficult to find a job, by reducing wage rates in black areas relative to white areas, or by increasing commuting costs. A more general statement of Kain's third hypothesis is, therefore, that the spatial mismatch between where blacks reside and where jobs are located reduces the net annual earnings of central city blacks.

It is important to understand the distinction between Kain's second and third hypotheses. Even in the absence of a spatial mismatch, involuntary housing segregation is expected to harm black workers. As Kain has noted, "...adding a constraint to any maximization problem must yield the result that a constrained population can do no better, and typically will do worse, than an unconstrained population" (1974, p. 10). However, the welfare loss experienced by blacks from housing segregation will obviously be greater if a spatial mismatch exists.

To investigate his hypotheses, Kain employed data from the Detroit Area Traffic Study of 1952 and the Chicago Area Traffic Study of 1956. Both cities were highly segregated. The proportions of the nonwhite population living in the city's principal ghetto were 93 and 96 percent for Detroit and Chicago, respectively. The following regression was estimated separately for each city:

$$W = \alpha + \beta R - \gamma D + e,$$

where W = percent of employment in the workplace zone held by blacks, where the workplace zone was defined as a small geographical area within the city;

   R = percent of total residents in the workplace zone who are black, which was included as a proxy for the degree of consumer discrimination in the zone; and

   D = distance between the center of the zone and the major black ghetto.

Kain found that R and W were directly related and that R and D were inversely related. Both effects were statistically significant at conventional levels for Chicago and Detroit. The negative sign on γ indicates that the racial composition of the workforce becomes less black as distance from the ghetto increases. The positive sign on β is consistent with the sheltered workplace hypothesis. According to Kain, "these findings would seem to suggest that housing market segregation does strongly affect the location of Negro employment"; that is, the evidence is taken as supportive of his first hypothesis.[3]

To investigate his second hypothesis, Kain used his regression results to predict the extent of black employment in each zone if the black population were spatially distributed evenly over all zones. By comparing these employment estimates to actual employment, he determined that the job loss to blacks attributable to residential segregation was 25,000 for Chicago and 9,000 for Detroit. Based on these findings, Kain concluded that housing market segregation does affect the level of black employment within metropolitan areas.

In testing his third hypothesis, Kain recognized that both jobs and white workers have suburbanized. As discussed above, the former is expected to harm the labor market position of blacks. The outmigration of whites, however, is expected to improve the job opportunities of blacks, since fewer whites would be competing against blacks for available central city jobs. So the question becomes, how do these offsetting trends net out? To obtain what he considered to be a crude indication of this, he solved the Chicago regression equations that were estimated for manufacturing employment, using the 1950 and 1960 values of R for each of the workplace zones. The estimated manufacturing employment ratios were then multiplied by total manufacturing employment in each of the zones in each of the years to obtain evidence of black manufacturing employment in 1950 and 1960. The results indicated that black employment declined by 4,000 to 7,000 jobs during the 10-year period, which is consistent with Kain's third hypothesis.

Soon after Kain published his article, his methodology was attacked in two comments, one by Offner and Saks (1971) and one by Masters (1974). Offner and Saks used Kain's data for Chicago to show that his results were highly sensitive to the form of the regression equation estimated. They regressed W on both R and R^2 and found that the quadratic term is statistically significant while the linear term is not. These results suggest that there is a threshold that must be exceeded before the black residential fraction has more than a nontrivial effect on black employment. When Offner and Saks used the results obtained from their quadratic equation to estimate the effects of ghetto dispersal on black employment, they found that this would cause large job *losses* for blacks. These results suggest that the increase in consumer discrimination resulting from residential dispersal would harm blacks more than the resulting improvement in job access would benefit them.

Masters' focus was on Kain's measure of the effect of housing segregation on the relative job opportunities of blacks, which is the predicted value of W (W^*) for each zone in the absence of housing segregation minus the actual value of W (W_A). He mathematically demonstrates that

$$W^* - W_A = -\hat{\gamma}\bar{D},$$

where $\hat{\gamma}$ is the estimated coefficient on the distance variable and $\bar{D}$ is the distance from the ghetto to the average zone. He argues that will be larger the greater the extent of housing segregation, and the absolute value of $\hat{\gamma}$ will be larger the greater the costs of transportation and reduced job information per unit of distance. The problem, according to Masters, is that the values of $\bar{D}$ and $\hat{\gamma}$ do not depend on the tightness of labor markets in black areas in comparison to white areas. As a result, Masters believes that "Kain has demonstrated no more in this part of his analysis than he had already demonstrated with regard to his first hypothesis – that housing segregation and transportation costs probably affect the distribution of Negro employment."

In summary, a fair assessment of Kain's article would be that he (1) advanced a number of hypotheses that warrant careful empirical investigation, and (2) provided some legitimate evidence in support of his first hypothesis – residential segregation affects the geographic distribution of black employment. That hypothesis, however, is much less interesting than his second and third, which deal with the level rather than the spatial distribution of black employment. The evidence he offers on these hypotheses, by his own admission, is much weaker and has been subject to multiple interpretations.

A Classification of Studies
Based Upon Their Methodological Approach

A wide variety of alternative empirical approaches have been employed to investigate Kain's hypotheses. Below I classify studies based upon the methodological approach utilized, summarize the results obtained from individual studies, and discuss the advantages and disadvantages of each methodology. For the sake of brevity, for each group I provide a table, giving the particulars of the individual studies — namely, data source, dependent variable, selected independent variables, and major findings. All known studies are reviewed, except those focusing exclusively on youth. The treatment of these studies is reserved for a later section.

Comparisons of Central City and Suburban Residents
Using Micro-Level Data

A number of studies have investigated Kain's third hypothesis by comparing the economic welfare of central city and suburban residents. (See table 2.1.) These comparisons arc based on the argument that blacks who live in the suburbs should have a significant advantage over otherwise comparable blacks who live in the central city, if blacks are significantly handicapped in the labor market by involuntary housing segregation.

All of the studies use microeconomic data drawn from a multiplicity of metropolitan areas and, with one exception, make welfare comparisons using one of two techniques. In some cases, the chosen measure of economic welfare is regressed on one or more dummy variables representing residential location, and controls for personal and, sometimes, metropolitan area characteristics. In other cases, separate equations are estimated for central city and suburban residents, which include the same types of control variables as in the single equation approach. Central city means are then substituted into the estimated suburban equations to predict the economic welfare of the average central city resident assuming he/she has moved to a suburban location.

Table 2.1 Comparisons of Central City and Suburban Residents Using Micro-Level Data

Author(s)	Data Source	Dependent Variable	Selected Independent Variables	Major Findings
Harrison (1972)	1966 Survey of Economic Opportunity data for the 12 largest SMSAs. Micro-data. Sample restricted to males.	Weekly earnings, unemployment rates, and occupational status.	Residential location: central city poverty area, rest of the central city, or suburban ring.	Frequency distributions of earnings, unemployment, and occupational status are very similar across residential locations for both blacks and whites.
Bell (1974)	1967 Survey of Economic Opportunity data for the 100 largest SMSAs. Sample restricted to married women.	Labor force participation and earnings.	Dummies for place for residence: central city poverty area, rest of central city, and the suburbs.	Blacks had the greatest labor force participation rates in the nonpoverty part of central city, rates were similar between suburbs and poor city areas. Earnings of suburban residents were lower than for those who lived in the nonpoor central city.
Vrooman and Greenfield (1980)	1973 data from National Opinion Research Corporation for the Adult Performance Level Project. Sample consisted of people aged 18 to 64, living in a	Sample stratified by race, sex, and residential location (central city versus suburban ring) and earnings equations estimated for each group.	Years of education, of vocational training, of work experience and a measure of functional competence.	Results indicated that as much as 40 percent of the earnings gap between white and black males could be eliminated by the dispersal of central city

	large number of different metro areas.			black males. The earnings gap for females would increase by 10 percent of black females dispersed.
Price and Mills (1985)	Current Population Survey for 1978. Sample restricted to fully employed males, aged 25 to 59, living in large SMSAs.	Annual earnings.	Residence in central city versus suburbs, personal and metropolitan area characteristics (the population, unemployment rate, and a set of regional amenity variables).	The concentration of blacks in central cities can at most explain 6 percent of lower black annual earnings out of a total difference of 34 percent.
Reid (1985)	National Longitudinal Survey for 1967 and 1977. Sample restricted to black and white women.	Hourly wage rate, separate equations estimated for each year.	Residential location (city versus suburbs), race, the characteristics of the individual and her metropolitan area (size of labor force and unemployment rate).	Results from equations that included controls for occupation and industry indicated that in both years the wages of black females were independent of residential location. In the absence of these controls, black females living in central cities were found to have a wage advantage in 1967 and a wage disadvantage in 1977.

Of the two, the latter technique is the preferable approach, since it permits both the intercept and the estimated coefficients on the control variables to vary between the central city and the suburbs.

Harrison (1972) was the first to make welfare comparisons based upon residential location. His is the only study reviewed in this section that does not rely upon regression analysis. Instead, he simply compared the frequency distributions of earnings, unemployment rates, and occupational status among male workers who resided in central city poverty areas, the rest of the central city, and the suburban ring. His results indicated that blacks living outside the poverty area, but within the central city, earned more than those living in the poverty area, but blacks living in the ring earned wages only comparable with nonpoverty area central city residents. Place of residence was found to have no effect on the number of weeks worked per year or the type of job held. Based upon his results, Harrison rejected Kain's hypothesis as an explanation for the labor market problems of blacks, and argued that it is racial discrimination in the labor market, not housing segregation, that limits the economic opportunities of blacks.

Bell (1974) conducted an analysis similar to Harrison's with the same data, but focused on married women rather than males. While his results were similar to those of Harrison, his methodology was an improvement, since equations were estimated that contained an extensive set of control variables. In these equations, earnings and labor force participation were alternatively regressed on dummy variables that represented the same residential locations used by Harrison. Bell's results suggested that black married women had the greatest labor force participation rates in the nonpoverty part of the central city, and that the rates were very similar between those living in the suburbs and the poor city areas. Regarding earnings, he found that suburban residents were in a worse state than those who lived in the nonpoor central city.

Vrooman and Greenfield (1980) went beyond earlier studies by actually computing how the suburban dispersal of the black population would affect the difference in earnings between the races. These computations were based upon the results obtained from earnings equations estimated separately for each race, sex, and residential location (i.e., central city versus suburban rings). Their results indicated that as much as 40 percent of the earnings gap between white and black males could be eliminated by the dispersal of central city black males. For females, however, they found that the earnings gap between the races would increase by roughly 10 percent if black females moved to the suburbs. No explanation was given for the divergent results obtained for males and females.

The studies reviewed thus far that have made welfare comparisons between central city and suburban residents are limited: characteristics of the metropolitan area that might affect individual economic performance were not included among the sets of independent variables, despite the fact that samples were drawn from groups of metropolitan areas. Since such variables have been shown to have important effects, omitted variables bias is a strong possibility. Price and Mills (1985) mitigate this problem by including an extensive set of metropolitan area descriptors in their estimated earnings equations. Like Vrooman and Greenfield, they estimate the portion of the earnings gap between whites and blacks that can be attributed to the fact that blacks are concentrated within central cities.

The results of Price and Mills sharply contrast with those of Vrooman and Greenfield. Price and Mills found that residential location could explain no more than 6 percent of the earnings gap between black and white males. Results for females were not provided. Like Harrison, they concluded that racial discrimination in the labor market is a much more important factor than housing segregation in explaining earnings differences between whites and blacks. It is important to keep in mind, however, that neither Harrison nor Price and Mills provides any direct evidence on the importance of discrimination. In both studies, it is the unexplained or residual difference in earnings between the races that is attributed to labor market discrimination. Since this residual may reflect many other differences between racial groups not entirely accounted for in the independent variables measurement, the conclusion of these studies that the influence of discrimination is dominant is open to question.

Like Bell, Reid (1985) restricted his analysis to the effect of residential location on the wages of black and white women. He motivates his study by making an important point that deserves attention in future work; namely, most previous studies dealing with job access issues have focused on the economic performance of males, despite the crucial role of black women in the lives of most black families. Reid regresses the natural log of the hourly wage rate on a set of dummy variables representing race and residential location—city versus suburbs—along with control variables describing the characteristics of the individual and the metropolitan area. Separate equations were estimated for 1967 and 1977. Results from equations, which included controls for occupation and industry, indicated that in both years the wages of black females were independent of residential location. However, in the absence of these controls, black females living in central cities were found to have a wage advantage in 1967 and a wage disadvantage in 1977. Reid concludes that his 1977 results are supportive of Kain's third hypothesis. He suggests that the difference in his results between the two years is attributable to more capable black females moving to the suburbs and taking suburban jobs over the 10-year period. No evidence is provided in support of this hypothesis. In addition, no explanation is given for the sensitivity of his results to the presence of occupation and industry in estimated equations. The reader is, therefore, not sure which set of results to believe.

In summary, the evidence obtained by making comparisons of the economic welfare of central city and suburban residents is highly contradictory. The results presented by Harrison and Price and Mills for males are inconsistent with those presented by Vrooman and Greenfield. For females, the results of Bell are consistent with those of Vrooman and Greenfield, but contrary to those obtained for 1977 by Reid. Unfortunately, no conclusion can be reached from reading this literature regarding whether suburban dispersal would improve the labor market position of central city blacks.

One possible explanation for this inconsistency is that comparisons of the welfare of central city and suburban residents provide, at best, a crude test of Kain's third hypothesis. Specifically, two serious shortcomings of this approach create biases that work against one another in potentially yielding any possible result. First, the residential location of the individual worker is treated as exogenous. The evidence is overwhelming that the worker's economic status affects his/her choice of location. Although a suburban residential location may increase economic welfare by offering superior job access, it is also true that people with jobs and higher earnings are more likely to self-select a suburban residence. The failure to account for this simultaneity between residential location and economic welfare means that suburban samples include economically successful blacks who hold jobs within the central city. In addition, suburban residents, wherever they hold jobs, are likely to possess unobserved productivity characteristics that positively correlate with earnings. For both of these reasons, comparisons by residential location will tend to bias results in favor of Kain's hypothesis.

A second limitation of these studies is the simple central-city–suburban-ring dichotomy used to define intrametropolitan residential location. This implicitly assumes that suburban employment growth uniformly improves—or fails to improve—the economic opportunities of all suburban households. Clearly, this has not been true for most metropolitan areas. Atlanta, for example, has experienced far greater employment growth in the northern rather than the southern suburbs. Atlanta's black suburban population, however, is concentrated on the south side on the fringe of the central city ghetto. The findings of Rose (1972) and Kain (1985) suggest that the location of suburban blacks in Atlanta is not atypical. They studied suburban communities with black majorities and determined that most growth occurred on the fringe of existing ghettos. If blacks tend to live in the relatively depressed areas of suburbia, a comparison of the welfare of suburban and central city blacks would bias results against Kain's hypothesis.

The results of an individual study will depend on how the aforementioned biases net out. The sign of the net bias will likely vary across samples consisting of different metropolitan areas and equations including different controls for the individual's productivity. It is, therefore, not surprising that welfare comparisons of central city and suburban residents have yielded such mixed results across studies.

Regressions of Black Economic Welfare on Measures of Job Decentralization and/or Housing Segregation

Studies in this category using aggregate data have been done by Mooney (1969), Friedlander (1972), Masters (1975), Galster (1987), and Farley (1987). (See table 2.2.) Ihlanfeldt and Sjoquist (1989) used microeconomic data. In general, the approach of these studies is to regress various measures of black economic welfare on variables computed at the metropolitan level, describing the extent of job decentralization and housing segregation. If housing segregation is found to have a negative effect, this would support Kain's second hypothesis. If job decentralization and black economic welfare are found to be inversely related, this would be consistent with Kain's third hypothesis.

The first study to employ this approach is Mooney's (1969). He regressed the ghetto employment rate—defined as the employment to population ratio—within each area on the metropolitanwide unemployment rate, the ratio of central city employment to total Standard Metropolitan Statistical Area (SMSA) employment in wholesale, trade, manufacturing, and services, and the proportion of nonwhites who live in the central city and work in the suburbs (a measure of accessibility to the suburban ring). In support of Kain's second and third hypotheses, he found that black employment rises with the fraction of blacks working in the suburbs and with the degree of job decentralization. He also found, however, that the magnitude of the effect of the SMSA unemployment rate was substantially greater than the effect of either the decentralization variable or the access to the ring variable. Based upon these results he concluded that macroeconomic policies designed to tighten labor markets were a better approach than suburban dispersal for improving the employment and income conditions of blacks.

Even less supportive of Kain's hypotheses are the results obtained by Friedlander (1972) and Masters (1975). Friedlander regressed central city and ghetto black unemployment rates on measures of housing segregation, the fraction of the metropolitan area's jobs located in the central city, and a group of control variables describing other characteristics of the SMSA. Similarly, Masters regressed the ratio of nonwhite-to-white median income for males on a variety of housing segregation indices, the percentage of SMSA jobs in the central city divided by the percentage of the SMSA population living in the central city, and the relative percentages of black and white males living and working in the SMSA who have suburban jobs. The latter two variables proxy the relative tightness of the central city labor market and the relative accessibility of suburban jobs to blacks and whites, respectively. In both of these studies, all of the variables related to Kain's hypotheses performed poorly and were seldom statistically significant with the expected sign at conventional levels. Friedlander's and Masters' results, therefore, failed to support Kain's second or third hypothesis.

Farley (1987) is the first author to use the methodological approach described in the section to generate strong evidence in favor of Kain's hypotheses. In addition, his study is the first to consider the effect of job access on the employment of Hispanics. The dependent variable in the equations estimated to study the problems of blacks is the ratio of the black male unemployment rate for the metropolitan area to the white male unemployment rate. The principal independent variables are (1) the percentage of the SMSA's jobs in manufacturing, retail trade, wholesale trade, and service industries located in the central city; and (2) the percentage of the SMSA's black population living in the central city. Where appropriate, Hispanic numbers were used in the construction of the variables in order to analyze the ratio of the Hispanic to the white unemployment rate. The results indicated that black and Hispanic male unemployment is higher relative to that of whites where jobs are more suburbanized and the minority population is the least so. These results lend support to Kain's second and third hypotheses.

Like the research comparing the economic welfare of central city and suburban residents, studies reviewed thus far that have regressed SMSA measures of black economic welfare on variables purporting to test Kain's hypotheses have yielded mixed results. The evidence provided by Mooney, and especially by Farley, tends to support Kain, while that of Masters and Friedlander does not. Once again, the methodological approach utilized by these studies has serious shortcomings.

First, all of the studies ignore the possibility that the extent of racial

Table 2.2 Regressions of Black Economic Welfare on Measures of Job Decentralization and/or Housing Segregation

Author(s)	Data Source	Dependent Variable	Selected Independent Variables	Major Findings
Mooney (1969)	1960 census data from 25 metro areas.	Ghetto employment rate (=employment-to-population ratio). Separate equations estimated for males and females.	The ratio of central city employment to total SMSA employment in wholesale, trade, manufacturing, and services; the metropolitan unemployment rate; the proportion of nonwhites who live in the central city and work in the suburbs.	Black employment found to rise with the fraction of blacks working in the suburbs and with the degree of job decentralization. But the effect of the SMSA unemployment rate was substantially larger than that for the decentralization or access to ring variables.
Friedlander (1972)	1960 census data for 75 metro areas.	Central city black unemployment rate and ghetto black unemployment rate.	Measures of housing segregation and the fraction of the metropolitan area jobs located in the central city.	Neither the segregation indices nor the job decentralization variable were found to have significant effects on black employment rates.
Masters (1975)	1960 Census of Population data for 65 SMSAs. Sample restricted to males.	Ratio of nonwhite to white median income.	Various housing segregation indices, the percentage of SMSA jobs that are in the central city divided by the percentage of the SMSA population living in the central city, and the relative percentages of black and white males living and working in the SMSA who have suburban jobs.	All of the variables related to Kain's hypotheses performed poorly and were seldom statistically significant with the expected sign.

Study	Data	Methodology	Variables	Findings
Farley (1987)	1980 Census of Population and Housing and 1977 Census of Industries. Sample restricted to black and Hispanic males.	Ratio of the minority male employment rate for the SMSA to the white male unemployment rate. Separate regressions were run for blacks and Hispanics.	The percentage of the SMSA population that is black (Hispanic); the percentage of the SMSA's jobs in manufacturing, retail trade, wholesale trade, and service industries located in central city; the percentage of the SMSA's black (Hispanic) population living in the central city; and the ratio of the percentage of blacks (Hispanics) who have graduated from high school to the percentage of whites who have done so.	Black and Hispanic male unemployment found to be higher relative to whites where jobs are more suburbanized and the minority population least so.
Galster (1987)	1970 Census of Population and the Department of Housing and Urban Development's 1977 Housing Markets Practices Survey.	A four equation model is estimated. The extent and centralized pattern of housing segregation and measures of black-white economic differences are treated as endogenous variables.	Variables that describe the SMSA's population, industrial structure, and labor and housing markets.	The results provide strong support for his simultaneous-equations specification and indicate the likely severe bias of previous studies. Housing segregation is found to significantly affect economic disparities between the races.
Ihlanfeldt and Sjoquist (1989)	Panel Study of Income Dynamics for 1978 merged with 1980 data from the Census of Population. Sample restricted to individuals who have no more than a high school degree and who live within a central city.	Individual's annual labor earnings minus total journey-to-work costs. Separate equations estimated for four race-sex groups.	Percentage of the SMSA's low-skill jobs located in the suburban ring, the individual's productivity characteristics; and metro area descriptors.	Job decentralization is found to have a substantial and equal negative effect on the net earnings of less-educated black and white males and lesser negative effect on the net earnings of females.

segregation and job decentralization within a particular metropolitan area is influenced by the aggregate economic welfare of the black population. In the first case, as economic welfare improves, blacks are known to leave the ghetto in search of higher quality housing, causing a reduction in housing segregation. In the second case, employers select suburban over central city locations, in part because the latter are perceived to be more crime-ridden, require the payment of higher taxes, and offer inferior schools. Since these problems can be linked to the aggregate economic welfare of central city blacks, job decentralization, like housing segregation, should be treated as an endogenous variable — i.e., a variable whose values need to be explained, rather than taken as given — when relying upon aggregate data.

One study that does not ignore the simultaneity between black economic welfare and racial segregation is Galster's (1987). To account for this simultaneity, he estimated a four-equation model. The extent and centralized pattern of housing segregation and measures of black-white economic differences were treated as endogenous variables. Exogenous variables, i.e., variables whose values were taken as given, describe the SMSA's population, industrial structure, and labor and housing markets. The results provided strong support for his simultaneous-equations specification and indicated the likely severe bias of previous studies. Housing segregation was found to significantly affect economic disparities between the races.

In addition to simultaneous-equations bias, another problem common to the above studies is that they incorrectly measure the decentralization of jobs, which normally will cause an underestimate of the effect of this variable on black economic welfare. To reliably test Kain's third hypothesis, job decentralization should be measured for only low-skill jobs, since the low educational attainment of most central city black workers qualifies them to hold only these jobs. Instead, studies have included all of the metropolitan area's jobs or summations of jobs across broad industrial classifications in computing the job decentralization variable.

The first study to use microeconomic data to investigate the relationship between black economic welfare and job decentralization was by Ihlanfeldt and Sjoquist (1989). Their individual-level data came from the Panel Study of Income Dynamics for the year 1978 and their SMSA-level variables were constructed using data from the 1980 Census of Population and Housing. The dependent variable, defined as the individual's annual labor earnings minus total journey-to-work costs, was designed to capture all of the ways in which job decentralization can disadvantage central city workers. It can reduce wage rate if wages are flexible, cause unemployment if wages are rigid, or lengthen the journey to work. Earnings net of transportation costs were regressed on the individual's productivity characteristics, the measure of job decentralization, and several other metropolitan area characteristics. The measure of job decentralization was defined as the percentage of the SMSA's low-skill jobs located in the suburban ring, where low-skill jobs are identified as those within occupational categories with low educational requirements.

The results indicated that job decentralization has a substantial and equal negative effect on the net earnings of less-educated black and white males and a lesser negative effect on the net earnings of females. A novel feature of this study is evidence from the estimation of a residential mobility model that suggests that the average white worker eventually relocates in response to a job-decentralization induced loss in earnings, while the average black worker does not. This result suggests that earning losses are more permanent for central city blacks and that black suburbanization is restricted by racial discrimination within the suburban housing market.

The Ihlanfeldt and Sjoquist study has a number of advantages over previous work. First, the use of microeconomic data permitted the inclusion of an extensive set of control variables, thus minimizing the possibility of simultaneous-equations bias in its results. Second, the comprehensive nature of the dependent variable is a better measure of black economic welfare than those employed in previous studies. Finally, the job decentralization variable measures the spatial distribution of only those jobs less-educated workers are likely to hold.

In summary, two studies that have taken the approach of regressing a measure of black economic welfare on variables related to Kain's hypotheses do not seem to be plagued by the methodological limitations of earlier work. The results of Galster support Kain's second hypothesis, while those of Ihlanfeldt and Sjoquist support his third hypothesis.

Comparisons of Wage Rates Paid by Work Location

In lieu of investigating the relationship between wage rates and residential location, a number of studies have tested Kain's hypotheses by comparing wage rates paid to blacks working in the central city to those paid to otherwise similar blacks working in the suburbs. (See table 2.3.) The results of these studies can be more informative than those that focus on residential location, but the proper interpretation of the results from these studies requires some theoretical background. There are three relevant theoretical models that can be labelled for ease of exposition: the wage-gradient model, the market-segmentation model, and the disequilibrium model.

A wage gradient shows the relationship between the wage rate and the distance the job is located from the central business district (CBD). The standard urban-land-use model predicts that the wage gradient will be negatively sloped. In other words, wage rates are expected to be lower for jobs located in the suburbs in comparison to the central city. Wage rates must be higher at worksites closer to the CBD to compensate workers for the higher cost of city housing or for the higher transportation cost incurred by commuting from more distant residential locations where housing costs are lower. The urban-land-use model assumes that locational choices are unconstrained. Workers, therefore, maximize their utility by selecting a residential location farther from the CBD than their job location and commute inward toward the CBD. The assumption of unconstrained residential location is less tenable in the case of blacks, however, since they are frequently excluded from suburban neighborhoods by the discriminatory behavior of housing suppliers.

If these exclusions are sufficiently strong, as White (1976, 1978, 1988) has noted, a suburban firm located at some distance from the CBD, say ten miles, may find an insufficient black labor supply farther out than the firm itself, and willing to work for the wage predicted ten miles from the CBD by the standard model. At this wage, the firm's

Table 2.3   Comparisons of Wage Rates Paid by Work Location

Author(s)	Data Source	Dependent Variable	Selected Independent Variables	Major Findings
Danziger and Weinstein (1976)	1970 Census of Employment Survey for Cleveland, Detroit, and St. Louis. Sample restricted to males, aged 21 to 64, who live in central city poverty areas.	Hourly earnings.	Wages are compared between workers who live and work in central city poverty areas and who live in the central city poverty areas but work in the suburban ring. The comparison is made by estimating an imputed wage for suburban workers from a regression of the wage of city workers on their individual characteristics, occupation, and industry. Comparisons are made for full sample and for whites, blacks, blue-collar workers, white-collar workers, operatives, and for each metro area.	No systematic differences are found between the wages of poverty area residents working in poverty areas and the suburban ring. Over half of the blacks commute to the suburbs and their wage net of commuting costs is less than what they would have earned in the central city.
Straszheim (1980)	1967 microdata from a household interview survey taken in San Francisco.	Annual household income. Sample is stratified by race and educational level.	A set of worksite dummies representing the ghetto, the nonghetto central city, and the suburbs. Control variables include age, whether the job is part time, and whether the individual is a supervisor.	The estimated coefficients on the worksite dummies suggest that wages decline with distance from the center of the city for white workers of all educational levels and for black workers with more than a high

Table 2.3   (*continued*)

Author(s)	Data Source	Dependent Variable	Selected Independent Variables	Major Findings
				school education. For blacks with less than a high school education a positive wage gradient is found.
Ihlanfeldt (1988)	1980 Public-Use Sample for the Atlanta SMSA.	Annual earnings. Separate equations are estimated for blacks and whites broken down by occupational category (service, blue-collar, and white-collar).	A set of worksite dummies representing the CBD, the rest of the central city, the inner suburbs, and the outer suburbs; and a vector of productivity variables.	For whites, the results suggest that a negative wage gradient exists for workers in blue-collar and white-collar jobs and a positive gradient exists for service workers. Blacks are found to have positive wage gradients, regardless of occupation.
Ihlanfeldt (forthcoming)	1980 Public-Use Sample for Philadelphia, Detroit, and Boston SMSAs.	Hourly wage rate. Samples are stratified by race and seven occupational groups. Separate equations are estimated for each stratification for each metro area.	Estimated distance in miles that the job is located from the CBD, and a vector of productivity variables.	Negatively sloped wage gradients are found for whites. For blacks, no relationship is found between the wage received and the distance the job is located from the CBD. Blacks are shown to make long commutes from the city to the suburbs.

| Hughes and Madden (1991) | 1980 Public-Use Sample for Cleveland, Detroit, and Philadelphia SMSAs. Sample restricted to male household heads working year round, full time. | Annual earnings net of rent and commuting costs. Net earnings are predicted for subcounty location zones from estimated wage and rent equations. | Wage equations include the standard set of human capital variables. Rent equations include structural characteristics and taste controls (income, marital status, occupation). | The welfare maximizing distribution of work and residential location is compared to the actual distribution of work and residential location to reach the following conclusions: (1) black residences are better located than white residence, given their respective job locations; (2) a change in job locations, given residential locations, would improve the welfare of blacks more than whites; and (3) considering both jobs and residences, blacks are less optimally located than whites. |

labor demand exceeds supply. To satisfy its labor requirements, this firm will have to raise wages in order to induce workers who live beyond a certain distance, perhaps five miles from the CBD, to outcommute. Firms at distances greater than ten miles from the CBD will have to pay correspondingly higher wage rates to compensate outcommuters for their longer commutes; hence, beyond five miles the wage gradient changes from negative to positive in slope.

Based upon the development of a model similar to White's, Straszheim (1980) concluded that the wage gradient for blacks may be positive throughout the metropolitan area because these workers remain concentrated in ghettos located within or close to the CBD. Straszheim's model predicts that wage gradients for blacks will rise and for whites will decline. These predictions are based on the assumption that black workers outcommute and white workers incommute. It is also necessary to assume that a finite elasticity of substitution exists between equally skilled black and white workers. Wage gradients can only differ between blacks and whites if race is a factor in hiring decisions.

The models of White and Straszheim assume that workers can find alternative employment within the central city, and therefore suburban employers must pay imported workers a compensating differential to cover their commuting costs. However, market imperfections, such as minimum wage laws and union rules, may prevent wages from falling to their equilibrium level within the central city. The existence of disequilibrium in the labor market implies that there will be a surplus of workers residing in the central city who will be forced to commute to the suburbs in order to find jobs. In this model, since suburban employers need not compensate imported workers from the central city for their commuting costs, the wage gradient for black workers is expected to be flat; that is, there should be no difference in the wages paid to blacks working in the central city and the suburbs.

Finally, there is the possibility that the metropolitan labor market is spatially segmented into central city and suburban submarkets. In this model, blacks residing in the central city are excluded from the suburban labor market by inadequate transportation facilities to meet the needs of reverse commuters and by racial discrimination on the part of suburban housing suppliers. Segmentation can result in lower wages and/or higher unemployment within the central city in comparison to the suburban ring.

In light of the above models, how do the results obtained from making wage comparisons by work location relate to Kain's hypotheses? If wages are found to be higher for blacks working in the suburbs, this would be consistent with both the White/Straszheim wage-gradient and labor-market-segmentation model. Since both models assume that black labor supply to suburban jobs is restricted by housing segregation, higher suburban wage rates would support Kain's first hypothesis.

If we knew that market segmentation was the cause of the higher suburban wage, the evidence would also be consistent with Kain's third hypothesis. It is difficult, however, to empirically distinguish between the wage-gradient and market-segmentation models. Information on commuting patterns would be suggestive, but not definitive. For example, if many blacks were found to be reverse commuters, this would tend to support the conclusion of the wage-gradient model that a wage differential in favor of the suburbs represents compensation for commuting costs.

Finally, if the difference in wages between the central city and the suburban ring is found to be small or nonexistent, this would be consistent with Kain's third hypothesis, but only if there is also evidence that this is the result of a surplus of black labor within the central city. The latter piece of evidence is necessary, since wage-rate similarity between areas may also reflect a labor market equilibrium where workers reside sufficiently close to their jobs that compensation for commuting costs is not required.

Danziger and Weinstein (1976) conducted the first study comparing the wages of blacks working in the central city and the suburban ring. Wages were compared between workers who live and work in central city poverty areas and those who live in central city poverty areas but work in the suburban ring. The comparison was made by estimating an imputed wage for suburban workers from the results of a regression of the wage of city workers on a set of individual characteristics and the occupation and industry classification of their jobs. The results indicated no systematic differences between the wages received by poverty area residents working in poverty areas and those working in the suburban ring. In addition, the study revealed that over half of the black poverty area residents commute to the suburbs and the wage net of commuting cost of the majority of these suburban workers is less than the net wage they would have earned by working in the central city. Danziger and Weinstein conclude that their results are consistent with what I have labelled the disequilibrium model and inconsistent with the wage-gradient and market-segmentation models.

Straszheim (1980) used data from a household interview survey taken in San Francisco to regress annual household income on a set of worksite dummies representing the ghetto, the nonghetto central city, and the suburbs. The sample was stratified by race and educational level, and separate regressions were run for each group. The estimated coefficients on the worksite dummies suggested that wages decline with distance from the center of the city for white workers of all educational levels and for black workers with more than a high school education. Straszheim suggests that for these groups of workers the basic commuting direction is toward the CBD, so that the negative wage gradient predicted by the standard urban land-use model is the expected result. For blacks with less than a high school education, a positive wage gradient was found. The latter piece of evidence is taken as support for his hypothesis that suburban employers must pay less-educated black workers a premium above what they could earn within the central city in order to induce them to reverse commute. Straszheim's results provide only weak support for his hypothesis, however, since he does not directly relate the wage rate to distance from the CBD and he provides no evidence on commuting behavior. There is the possibility, therefore, that market segmentation accounts for his results.

Straszheim's regressions were marred by the use of household income—rather than worker's earnings as his dependent variable, small sample sizes, and few control variables. These problems were not encountered by Ihlanfeldt (1988), who estimated earnings equations with data from the 1980 Public-Use Sample for Atlanta. Separate equations, broken down by occupational category (service workers, blue-collar workers, and white-collar workers), were estimated for blacks and whites. Following Straszheim's approach, dummy variables indicating where the worker worked within the metropolitan area were included among the set of independent variables: the CBD, the rest of the central city, the inner suburbs, and the outer suburbs. For whites, the results suggested that a negative wage gradient exists for workers in blue-collar and white-collar occupations and a positive wage gradient exists for service workers. For blacks, all three occupational groups were found to have positive wage gradients. While the spatial pattern in wage rates across work areas observed for blacks was strongly consistent with the White/Straszheim wage-gradient model, once again supplementary evidence that would have ruled out the possibility of market segmentation was not provided. The results of both Straszheim and Ihlanfeldt, therefore, provide unambiguous evidence only in support of Kain's first hypothesis.

The studies reviewed thus far in this section have investigated differences in the average wage paid across large intraurban work areas. Ihlanfeldt (forthcoming) is the first study to directly relate black and white wage rates to the distance, in miles, that the job is located from the CBD. The results indicated that wage gradients are negatively sloped for white workers. This is the expected result, since his evidence on commuting patterns indicates that white workers, regardless of their occupation, commute inward toward the CBD to work. For blacks, the evidence on commuting patterns indicates that (1) they are on net outcommutes from the central city; (2) the representative outcommuter makes a considerable commute; and (3) large numbers of central city blacks work in the suburbs.[5] The wage equations for blacks revealed *no* statistically significant relationship between the wage received and the distance the job is located from the CBD; hence, despite their long commutes, blacks were not found to earn more outside the central city. The only reasonable explanation for this finding is that a surplus of black labor exists within the central city. The commuting and wage evidence provided by Ihlanfeldt provides strong support for the disequilibrium model and, therefore, for Kain's third hypothesis.

Hughes and Madden (1991) attempted to account not only for the effect of job location on wages, but also the effect of residential location on housing costs, and the effect of job and residential location on commuting costs. They first estimated housing rent and wage equations for subcounty location zones for each of the metropolitan areas included in their analysis. These results were then used to predict the wage rate and housing rent of the individual at each location given his personal characteristics and the characteristics of his dwelling unit. Annual commuting costs were estimated between specific residential and job locales based upon the daily commuting times observed for individuals who actually commuted between these locales.

Given the predicted wage, rent, and commuting cost for each location, they computed a measure of the expected economic welfare of each individual at each location. The welfare measure was defined as earnings net of rent and commuting costs. The welfare maximizing distribution of work and residential location was compared to the actual distribution of work and residential location to reach the following conclusions: (1) black residences are better located than white residences, given their respective job locations; (2) a change in job locations, given residential locations, would improve the welfare of blacks more than whites; and (3) considering both jobs and residences, blacks are no less optimally located than whites within the metropolitan area. Their explanation for these results is that blacks live in relatively low-rent areas that offset their relatively low wage (net of commuting costs) employment locations.

Since the results of Hughes and Madden show that blacks could earn higher net wages if they worked in the suburbs rather than the central city, this evidence is consistent with Kain's third hypothesis. Taken alone, such evidence would imply that black economic welfare would be improved by suburban dispersal. However, what Hughes and Madden purport to show is that if blacks moved both their jobs and residences to the suburbs the increase in wages would be entirely offset by the need to pay more for housing of the same type they had previously occupied within the central city. This is the logic underlying their third conclusion.

The validity of the conclusions reached by Hughes and Madden hinge upon the reliability of their housing-cost and wage-rate predictions for each location zone. Their wage equations included the standard set of worker characteristics and, therefore, probably provide reasonably accurate wage-rate predictions. There is little reason, therefore, to question the evidence, which is consistent with Kain's third hypothesis. Due to the limitations of the data, however, their housing rent equations included only the structural characteristics of the dwelling unit and a number of taste controls, such as income, marital status, and occupation. Neighborhood and public service characteristics, which are known to affect rents, could not be included. Since these characteristics are likely to be less desirable within black areas, their predictions of lower housing rents for blacks, in comparison to whites, may be the result of the underspecification of their rent equations. There is ample reason to question, therefore, their conclusion that blacks would pay more for housing if they moved to the suburbs. Nevertheless, Hughes and Madden have raised an important issue that deserves careful attention in future work. If their results are confirmed by analysis based on better data, they would lend support to Hughes' (1987, 1989a, 1989b) contention that the welfare of central city blacks can be most improved by subsidizing their commute to suburban jobs rather than by moving them to suburban neighborhoods. This, however, is a contentious issue, which I will take up at greater length in chapter 5.

Our review of studies that have compared wages by work location yields two conclusions. First, the evidence presented in these studies provides consistent support for Kain's first and third hypotheses. Second, a wage-rate differential in favor of the suburbs exists for some metropolitan areas but not for others. An explanation for these divergent findings is that a positive wage gradient for blacks will only exist if blacks can find alternative employment within the central city. This is expected to vary among central cities, and also over time for particular central cities, depending upon existing economic conditions.

The Use of a Direct Measure of Job Accessibility

Another approach to exploring Kain's hypotheses is to relate the economic performance of individuals residing within a single metropolitan area to an intra-metropolitan measure of job accessibility. (See table 2.4.) For example, if job access affects employment and blacks have poorer access to jobs than whites, then part of the employment rate differential between the races can be attributed to housing segregation. Such a finding would support Kain's third hypothesis.

The problem with this approach is that while job access may affect employment, having a job may also affect the magnitude of the measure of job access. For example, people with jobs may choose to reside in areas with poor proximity to jobs in order to consume more housing at a lower price. This explanation is supported by considerable empirical evidence showing that commute times rise with the level of income.[5] If the simultaneity between employment and residential location is ignored, the estimated effect of job access on employment will be biased toward zero.

Two approaches might be taken to overcome the simultaneity problem between employment and residential location, and thereby provide reliable estimates of the job access effect on the probability of employment: (1) a system of equations is estimated that treats both employment and job access as endogenous variables; or (2) the analysis is restricted to those individuals whose residential location can legitimately be considered as exogenous. Although the first approach is preferred, the data requirements exceed those currently available; therefore, the studies that have used a direct measure of job access have either ignored the simultaneity problem or restricted the analysis to youths still living at home. Since it is unlikely that the employment status of the teenager has much of an influence on where his/her parents chose to reside, simultaneity between the youth's job probability and the measure of job access should not be a problem. Youth studies that have used measures of job access are reviewed in the next section. Studies that have ignored the simultaneity problem are reviewed below.

Hutchinson (1974, 1978) conducted the first studies that used a direct measure of job access. His first article focused on the relationship between job access and employment, while the second dealt with the relationship between job access and labor force participation. His samples consisted of household heads residing in 85 poverty zones located in

Table 2.4   The Use of Direct Measure of Job Accessibility

Author(s)	Data Source	Dependent Variable	Selected Independent Variables	Major Findings
Hutchinson (1974, 1978)	1967 household survey by the Southwestern Pennsylvania Regional Planning Commissoin for Pittsburgh SMSA. Samples consist of household heads residing in 85 traffic-analysis zones.	Employment and labor force participation probabilities. Separate equations estimated for each race and location (central city versus suburbs).	Job access within the residential zone, which is measured as the number of jobs within a reasonable commute of the zone; index of housing segregation; and productivity variables.	Job access is found to have a small positive effect on both the probability of employment and labor force participation.
Leonard (1986a)	Census tract data from the 1980 Census of Population and Housing for Los Angeles and Orange Counties. Information on the geographic distribution of jobs is added to census tracts from the 1974 and 1978 Equal Employment Opportunity Surveys.	Mean commuting time and employment rates for the census tract.	The number of jobs within a 15-minute commute of each census tract divided by the population 16 years of age and older of the commuting zone; the racial composition of the tract.	Blacks are found to have longer commutes even after controlling for job access. Job access has a small positive effect on the employment rate of teenagers, but no effect on adults. Dominant explanatory variable is racial composition of the tract.

the Pittsburgh metropolitan area. As the measure of job access, he used the number of jobs, of all types, that could be found within a reasonable commuting time of the zone. Blacks were found to have worse access to jobs than whites. As one might expect, his labor force and employment equations yielded almost identical results. Across all equations, the measure of job accessibility is statistically significant, but its effect is so small in magnitude that economic significance is not suggested.

Hutchinson's analysis can be criticized on two accounts. First, his measure of job access is likely to be a poor proxy for the actual number of jobs available to the average black worker residing within a poverty area. As I have already emphasized, most of these workers do not compete for all types of jobs, but only for those requiring little education or training. In addition, if job seekers who live within the commuting area are numerous relative to the number of jobs, then job access may be poor, even in those areas where the absolute number of jobs is large. Second, as stated above, Hutchinson ignores the simultaneity that exists between employment and residential location. Both of these shortcomings suggest that his estimates probably understate by a considerable margin the importance of job accessibility on black employment.

Leonard (1986a) estimated both commuting-time and employment rate equations at the census tract level for the Los Angeles metropolitan area. He found that mean commuting time is higher in census tracts containing more blacks. To determine whether this is caused by poor job access, he regressed mean commuting time on a host of variables including, as the measure of job access, the number of jobs within a 15-minute commute of each census tract, divided by the population 16 years of age and older in the commuting zone. The results indicated that blacks have longer commutes, even after controlling for job accessibility. Leonard suggests that this is due to labor market discrimination, which causes blacks to search farther afield to find jobs. He contends that higher commuting time for blacks is not explained by the spatial mismatch hypothesis.

In his second set of equations, the employment rate for the census tract was regressed on the job access measure, the percentage of the tract that is black, and other variables. He found that job access has a small positive effect on the employment rates of teenagers, but no effect on adults. The dominant explanatory variable in all equations was the racial composition of the census tract. As the percent of blacks rises, the employment rate declines; moreover, the importance of race was largely unaffected by the inclusion of the job access measure. Based upon his results, Leonard concluded that the spatial mismatch hypothesis is not an important explanation for high unemployment rates among urban blacks.

Leonard's analysis is limited by his failure to account for the simultaneity between employment and residential location. In addition, while his measure of job accessibility is an improvement over Hutchinson's, in that it accounts for both the number of jobs and the number of competitors within the commuting area, it is far from ideal. In particular, like Hutchinson's measure, it implicitly assumes that all workers, regardless of their qualifications, compete for the same jobs within the commuting area. The problem is not that blacks are distant from jobs, but rather that they are distant from the jobs they would be qualified to hold. For example, the jobs-to-population ratio is high for blacks living near the CBD, but most CBD jobs require a level of training or education that excludes black workers.

Interracial Comparisons of Commuting Times and Distances

If blacks are more distant from jobs than whites, this could cause black commuting times and distances to be either shorter or longer than those of comparable whites. On the one hand, commutes may be shorter for blacks, if they cannot afford long commutes or if information on job openings declines with distance. On the other hand, blacks may have longer commutes if they travel to more distant jobs. Two studies have investigated Kain's hypotheses by comparing the commuting times and distances of nonwhite and white workers. (See table 2.5.)

Greytak (1974) argues that housing segregation will decrease the employment of black secondary workers (e.g., women and teenagers), because these workers will be less willing or able to commute to distant jobs. For married adult males, however, he suggests that the costs of

Table 2.5   Interracial Comparisons of Commuting Times and Distances

Author(s)	Data Source	Dependent Variable	Selected Independent Variables	Major Findings
Greytak (1974)	Personal interviews conducted in 1965 by the Survey Research Center at the University of Michigan. Sample is representative of male heads of households living in the metropolitan U.S.	Distance in miles of the work trip. Separate equations estimated for four size classes of metropolitan areas.	Race of worker (white versus nonwhite), mode of transportation, whether trip originated in central city.	For SMSAs larger than three million, nonwhites are found to commute six miles farther than whites. No significant racial differences are found for smaller SMSAs.
Gordon et al. (1989)	Nationwide Personal Transportation Studies for 1977 and 1983–1984.	Travel times and distances to work.	No regressions are run, only comparisons of means.	White and nonwhite manufacturing workers are found to have similar commutes.

isolation from major places of work are likely to take the form of time-consuming worktrips.

Because of data constraints, Greytak was not able to compare the commutes of blacks and whites, so his comparisons were between nonwhites and whites. His sample was representative of male heads of households living in the metropolitan United States. Commuting distances between whites and nonwhites living in metropolitan areas with fewer than three million in population were found to be small and statistically insignificant. In SMSAs with more than three million in population, however, nonwhites were found to commute six miles farther than whites, and this difference was highly significant. Based upon these results, Greytak concluded that residential segregation and employment decentralization have interacted in a manner to cause nonwhite working heads of households to make a relatively time-consuming and protracted journey to work. The evidence, therefore, tends to support Kain's third hypothesis.

In a much more recent study, Gordon et al. (1989) compared travel times and distances among many different groups of workers. The comparisons directly relating to Kain's hypotheses are those presented for white versus nonwhite manufacturing workers. These comparisons lead Gordon and his colleagues to conclude that whites and nonwhites have similar commutes; therefore, the evidence does not offer firm support for the spatial mismatch hypothesis. The analysis, however, is plagued by data and conceptual problems. First, mean distances and times were computed separately for central city and suburban residents, and interracial comparisons were made for each area. These comparisons shed little light on Kain's hypotheses, however, since they do not capture interarea differences in job accessibility. If blacks are concentrated within the central city where jobs are scarce and whites are found predominantly in the suburban ring where jobs are plentiful, then the issue is whether there is a commuting-time difference between blacks and whites for the entire metropolitan area. Second, many of their comparisons were based on extremely small samples, since mean distances and times were computed as long as 10 cases were available.

The Use of Establishment-Level Data

Two studies feature a methodological approach that cannot be placed into any of the categories identified above. (See table 2.6.) They are reviewed together in this subsection only because they both rely on establishment-level data. Their methodological approaches are quite different.

Leonard (1987) regressed a firm's share of blue-collar jobs held by blacks on the distance the firm is located from the ghetto and on a vector of establishment characteristics that measured affirmative action pressures and skill requirements. Both level and change equations were estimated. His findings indicated that distance from the main ghetto is one of the strongest and most significant determinants of levels and changes in the racial composition of the workforce. Support is, therefore, provided for Kain's first hypothesis.

Leonard also presented evidence demonstrating that although the average blue-collar job moved farther from the ghetto in Chicago, and ghetto jobs disappeared, the average black employed in a blue-collar job worked closer to the ghetto. Leonard interprets this evidence as offering support for the hypothesis that housing segregation limits the employment opportunities of blacks, i.e, Kain's second hypothesis. This evidence is only suggestive, however, since the tendency of blacks to work closer to home may also result from competing white workers shifting their labor supply from the city to the suburbs as jobs decentralize.

Zax and Kain (1991) argue that if residential location decisions are unconstrained, then residential moves will occur if commutes are too short, and quits will occur if commutes are too long. Quits and moves by workers whose residential locations are constrained by housing segregation, however, should be relatively insensitive to commutes. To investigate their hypothesis, they estimated simultaneous-probit models of the move and quit decisions, using information from the payroll records of an unidentified service firm located in the Detroit SMSA.

In addition to commuting time, the move and quit equations contained an extensive set of control variables that theory suggests should affect these decisions. For whites, the effects of commutes on move and quit

Table 2.6 The Use of Establishment-Level Data

Author(s)	Data Source	Dependent Variable	Selected Independent Variables	Major Findings
Leonard (1987)	Equal Employment Opportunity establishment level data for Los Angeles and Chicago for the years 1974 and 1980. Sample consists only of males.	Fraction of establishment employment held by blacks. Both level and change equations were estimated.	Distance the firm is located from the ghetto; vector of establishment characteristics that measured affirmative action measures and skill requirements.	Distance from the main ghetto is found to be a strong determinant of levels and changes in the racial composition of the workforce.
Zax and Kain (1991)	Information from the payroll records of an unidentified service firm located in the Detroit SMSA.	Residential-move and job-quit probabilities. Separate equations estimated for whites and blacks.	Commuting time and an extensive set of control variables that theory suggests should affect move and quit decisions.	For whites, the effects of commutes on move and quit propensities are statistically significant with the anticipated signs. Commute effects are insignificant in the black equations. Results support the hypothesis that quits and moves by workers whose residential locations are constrained by segregation are insensitive to commutes.

propensities were statistically significant with the anticipated signs. For blacks, the expected result of no significant commute effects in either equation was obtained. The results of Zax and Kain illustrate that housing segregation reduces the economic welfare of blacks by forcing them to accept a suboptimal commute. While whites can adjust their commute to the optimal level by quitting or moving, blacks cannot. Support is therefore provided for Kain's second hypothesis.

Job Accessibility and Youth Employment

A number of studies have focused exclusively on the effect of job accessibility on youth employment. (See table 2.7.)[*] Several factors explain the special attention given to this group. First, racial differences in employment rates and unemployment rates are larger for youths than for the adult population. Second, there is more policy interest in black youth joblessness because of its relationship to crime and scarring. Recall the scarring hypothesis: if youths are unable to develop on-the-job skills and work attitudes, they experience relatively lower wages and higher unemployment as they grow older. Finally, youths provide an interesting test case for Kain's hypotheses. For this group, commuting is more difficult, labor market information is less perfect, and residential relocation is less affordable. The job access effect on black employment, therefore, should be particularly strong among youths. In addition, as noted above, possible simultaneity between employment status and the measure of job access is a lesser concern, since most youths are still living at home.

Osterman (1980) was interested in testing Kain's third hypothesis as well as the hiring-queue hypothesis as explanations for the high level of black youth joblessness. According to the latter hypothesis, employers have a preference for hiring white youths and adult women over black youths, which reduces black employment in those labor markets where the labor force includes relatively large numbers of preferred workers. Osterman estimated regression models separately for white and black teenagers. The dependent variables in his multiple-equation model were the rate of employment, the rate of labor force participation, and the rate of school enrollment, all measured for the metropolitan area. Included among his set of independent variables were the number of adult women in the labor force as a percentage of total employment, the number of white or black youths in the labor force as a percentage of total employment, and the ratio of jobs in the central city to suburban jobs, divided by the ratio of the population of the central city to the population of the suburbs. His results lead him to conclude that a small part of the differential labor market experience of white and black youths is due to the competition black youths encounter from women and white youths. No support was found for Kain's hypothesis.

Osterman recognized that his equations were marred by the omission of control variables measuring individual differences among youths. Perhaps a more serious limitation that he did not recognize was the crudeness of his job access measure. While it can be criticized on a number of accounts, its most glaring shortcoming is that it is based upon the spatial distribution of all of the jobs within the metropolitan area rather than the locations of just entry-level or low-skilled jobs suitable for teenagers.

In recent years, the most frequently cited study that has investigated the effect of job access on black employment is Ellwood (1986). He implemented three different empirical methodologies using data for the Chicago metropolitan area. His first approach involved using census tracts as the unit of observation to estimate employment rate equations. The dependent variable was the employment rate for 16 to 21-year-old, out-of-school youths living in the census tract. The key independent variables were the percentage of the tract's population who were black, and three alternative measures of job access. The access measures were computed for each of 116 "community zones" that exhaust the total land area of the Chicago SMSA. They were defined as follows: (1) the number of jobs within a 30-minute rapid transit commute of the zone; (2) the number of jobs located within the zone, divided by the number of people residing in the zone; and (3) the average journey-to-work time for workers living in the zone. None of the job access measures was found to have an important influence on the employment rate, and the estimated

Table 2.7 Job Accessibility and Youth Employment

Author(s)	Data Source	Dependent Variable	Selected Independent Variables	Major Findings
Osterman (1980)	SMSA-level census data for 1960 and 1970 for 54 SMSAs.	The dependent variables in his multiple-equation model are the rate of employment, the rate of labor force participation, and the rate of school enrollment. Separate models estimated for white and black 16 to 19-year-olds.	Number of adult women and white (black) youth in the labor force as a percentage of total employment; ratio of jobs in the central city to suburban jobs divided by the ratio of the population of the suburbs.	Decentralization of jobs relative to workers is not found to effect youth employment. Small part of the differential labor market experience of white and black youth is attributed to the competition black youth encounter from women and white youth.
Ellwood (1986)	1970 census tract data for Chicago SMSA; 1970 Chicago Area Transportation Study.	Census tract employment rate for out-of-school 16 to 21-year-olds.	Percentage of the tract's population that is black, Spanish-speaking, poor, and under 25 years old; three different measures of job access computed for each of 116 community zones: (1) the number of jobs within a 30-minute rapid transit commute of the zone; (2) the number of jobs located within the zone divided by the number of	None of the job access measures is found to have an important influence on the employment rate and the estimated coefficient on percent black is unaffected by their inclusion.

			people in the zone; and (3) the average journey-to-work time for workers living in the zone.	
Ihlanfeldt and Sjoquist (1990)	1980 Public-Use Microdata Sample for Philadelphia SMSA	Employment probability. Separate equations are estimated for blacks and whites broken down by age, whether the youth still lived at home; and enrollment status.	Job access measures are computed for 26 residential zones. Principal measure of job access is the mean travel time of low-wage workers who travelled to work by private, motorized carrier and who lived in the same residential zone as the youth. Separate times computed for blacks and whites.	Job access is found to have a strong effect on the job probabilities of white and black youth. From one-third to one-half of the racial gap in youth employment rates is attributable to job access, depending on the group.
Ihlanfeldt and Sjoquist (1991a)	1980 Public-Use Microdata for 43 SMSAs. Samples are restricted to teenagers who lived at home within central cities.	Employment probability. Separate equations estimated for blacks and whites.	Mean travel time for low-wage workers living within the central city; metropolitan labor market descriptors (unemployment rate of prime-age males, adult females as a percentage of the labor force).	For both races, travel time is found to have a strong effect on job probability.

coefficient on percent black was unaffected by their inclusion. These results suggest that racial differences in employment rates do not result from whites enjoying superior job proximity.

Ellwood's second test of the job access hypothesis involved substituting community zone dummy variables for the measures of job access in his employment rate equations. The estimated coefficient on percent black increased, which indicates that intrazonal racial differences in employment rates are larger than interzonal differences, *ceteris paribus*. Since job access is presumably quite similar for blacks and whites within the same zone, these results were interpreted as reinforcing those obtained with the measures of job access.

His final test of the job access hypothesis was to conduct "natural experiments," which compared the labor market outcomes of blacks who live on the South and West sides of Chicago and the outcomes of blacks and whites who live on the West side. All of Ellwood's measures of job access and his own casual observation, gained while driving through the areas, indicated that the West side provides much better access to jobs than the South side. His comparisons of black men, aged 16 to 21, living in low-income census tracts on the South and West sides revealed little difference between the two groups in their unemployment rates, employment rates, or educational attainment. In contrast, his comparisons between black and white out-of-school men, living in poor census tracts on the West side, revealed large differences in unemployment rates and employment rates in favor of whites. These results, along with those obtained from his employment-rate equations, all supported his frequently repeated aphorism: "Thus, the problem isn't space. It's race."

The robustness of Ellwood's findings across three different methodologies would seem to go a long way toward ending the debate over the role of job access as a cause of high joblessness among black youths. The reliability of each of his separate tests of the job access hypothesis, however, is open to question. His regressions of employment rates on measures of job access can be criticized on two accounts. First, Leonard (1986a) has suggested that the poor performance of the job access measures may reflect measurement error, since their construction was based on small samples. Second, the endogeneity of residential location with respect to employment status was ignored. As noted above, simultaneous-equations bias implies that the estimated coefficients on his job access measures are biased toward zero.

His fixed effects employment rate equation, which showed a large racial difference in employment rates within zones, can be criticized for inadequately accounting for individual and family differences between white and black youths that may account for this difference. Finally, his natural experiments may be unreliable because they too were based on small sample sizes and provided no controls for individual differences. Furthermore, Kasarda (1989) provides evidence contrary to Ellwood's assertion that the West side of Chicago provides better job access to black youth than the South side.

In contrast to the results of Leonard (reviewed above in the classification section), Osterman, and Ellwood, our previous work has suggested that poor job access is a significant contributor to the joblessness of black youths (Ihlanfeldt and Sjoquist 1990 and 1991a). In our first study, the 1980 Public-Use Sample for the Philadelphia metropolitan area was used to estimate job-probability equations for white and black youths. The measure of job access was the mean travel time of low-wage workers, who travelled to work by private, motorized carrier and lived in the same residential zone as the individual youth. The estimated partial derivatives of job probability, with respect to travel time, were statistically significant and nontrivial in magnitude for both races. For whites, a one standard deviation increase in travel time was found to reduce the probability of having a job by 3.8 to 5.1 percentage points, depending on the group considered. The corresponding range for blacks was 4.0 to 6.3 percentage points. A partial decomposition analysis (Oaxaca 1973; Blinder 1973) was conducted to determine how much of the difference in black and white employment rates could be attributed to blacks having poorer access to jobs than whites. These results indicated that the range in the amount of the racial gap in employment rates attributable to job access was roughly one-third to one-half, depending on such factors as the functional form of the estimated equations and the age group considered.

Additional results were obtained for Los Angeles and Chicago. These two metropolitan areas were selected, because they were the ones studied by Leonard and Ellwood, respectively. The limitations of the data prevented us from calculating separate mean travel times for whites and blacks.[6] While this prevented us from conducting a decomposition analysis, the results did indicate that higher mean travel times, computed for low-wage workers of all races, are associated with lower black employment rates in both Chicago and Los Angeles.

In our second study, samples were restricted to teenagers living within 43 central cities. The probability of the teenager having a job was regressed on travel time, individual and family background variables, and variables describing the prevailing conditions within the metropolitan area labor market. The estimated partial derivatives of job probability with respect to travel time were once again found to be statistically significant for blacks and whites and nontrivial in magnitude.

The fact that we found job access to be an important determinant of youth employment, while previous studies have not, may reflect a number of improvements in our chosen methodology. First, our measures of job access were designed specifically to capture the nearness of jobs available to youths, namely, low-wage jobs or jobs more frequently held by teenagers). Second, by focusing our analysis on youths still living at home, our estimates should not be plagued by simultaneous-equations biases. Finally, our use of microeconomic data enabled us to estimate separate equations for blacks and whites, which included variables describing the major individual and family characteristics most likely to affect youth employment. There is, therefore, a lesser concern that unobserved heterogeneity between the races has confounded our results.

Conclusions

This chapter has reviewed 30 studies that have presented evidence relevant to one or more of Kain's hypotheses. The evidence provides consistent support for Kain's first hypothesis: residential segregation affects the geographical distribution of black employment. However, the evidence on his second hypothesis, that housing segregation reduces black economic welfare, and his third, that there exists a mismatch between where blacks reside and where jobs are located, is highly contradictory. From a public policy perspective, there would seem to be no firm basis for recommending policies to improve the job accessibility of poor urban blacks; however, many of the studies reviewed in this chapter have been criticized for employing a flawed methodology. These flaws have frequently resulted in estimated effects that suffer from simultaneous-equations and errors-in-variables biases. If we dismiss the studies obviously plagued by one or both of these problems and focus only on the remaining research, the empirical evidence is no longer contradictory; rather, it provides strong and consistent support for Kain's second and third hypotheses.

In the next two chapters, I provide additional support for the hypothesis that job access affects the job probabilities of urban youth and that differences in job accessibility are important in explaining differences in employment rates among various groups. The research presented in these chapters extends our earlier work in two important directions. First, chapter 3 addresses the issue of whether or not the strong job access effects found in our earlier work are general phenomena. Separate estimates of the importance of job access to youth employment are provided for many different groups, defined on the basis of residential location, family income, race, and school enrollment status.

Second, our previous work and the research presented in chapter 3 assumes that school enrollment is exogenously determined. In chapter 4, I relax this assumption and provide estimates of the joint impact of intraurban job accessibility on the enrollment and employment decisions of teenagers. The motivation underlying this analysis is twofold. First, from a policy perspective it is crucial to determine whether job access affects a youth's decision to drop out of school. Second, it is obviously of interest to determine how the magnitude of the job access effect on employment is affected when school enrollment is treated as an endogenous variable.

NOTES

[1] The recent resurgence of interest in job access issues can be attributed to the worsening economic conditions of less-educated central city black residents, despite considerable growth in the national economy during the 1980s. The suburbanization of low-skill jobs and continued housing market segregation are well-recognized facts that suggest that a decline in job accessibility may be at least partially responsible for these conditions.

[2] Yinger (1979) provides the most comprehensive and thorough review of the literature on racial discrimination in the housing market. He concludes that the evidence "overwhelmingly supports the proposition that racial discrimination is a powerful force in urban housing markets." The most convincing evidence that supports Yinger's conclusion are the results obtained from fair-housing audits. These audits involve a white visiting a real estate office or rental complex in a simulated search for housing. Either shortly before or after the visit of this white auditor, a black auditor of the same sex and age also visits this real estate office or rental complex. Both auditors request the same type of unit and provide the same answers to questions dealing with family size, income, or related matters. In the 15 or so studies completed by investigative journalists and other groups (for example, the U.S. Department of Housing and Urban Development) of which I am aware, blacks are typically given different information than whites on whether housing is available about one out of every three visits.

[3] In addition to defining W as the percent of black employment in the zone held by blacks, Kain estimated separate equations for different industry and occupational groups. These results were consistent with those obtained using total employment.

[4] For example, in the case of Detroit, approximately 40,000 blacks living within the central city commuted to the suburbs to work in 1980. Ninety-one percent of these workers travelled by automobile, and the mean one-way commuting time was 31 minutes. Twenty percent of these auto travellers had commutes that took at least 45 minutes. The 9 percent of outcommuters who relied on public transit took on average 50 minutes to get to work.

[5] See, for example, Ellwood (1986) tables 4.2 and 4.3.

[6] The Philadelphia analysis was based on sample A (5 percent) of the Public-Use Sample. The B sample (1 percent) was used for Los Angeles and Chicago, because for these metropolitan areas the B sample provides much greater spatial disaggregation than does the A sample.

3

Empirical Evidence on the Effect of Intraurban Job Accessibility on Youth Employment

The location of jobs *vis-à-vis* the youth's residence can impinge on his/her probability of having a job for two distinct reasons. First, as the required commuting distance increases, the wage net of travel expense declines, which decreases the likelihood that the net wage will exceed the youth's reservation wage, i.e., the lowest possible wage that the youth would accept. In comparison to workers earning a higher wage, this effect may be particularly strong for typical teenagers, since for any given distance, travel costs are a higher percentage of their earnings and their travel time is greater because they more frequently must rely on slower modes of transportation, for example, walking, bicycling, or busing. Second, as documented by Holzer (1987), for both white and black youths, the most frequently used methods of job search are checking with friends and relatives and applying directly without referrals. Reliance on these informal methods of search suggests that a youth's information on available job opportunities may decay rapidly with distance from home.

Reservation wages, transportation costs per unit distance, and job market information vary among individual youths, depending on such factors as residential location, family income, enrollment status, and race. This implies that the effect of distance between a youth's residential location and the location of available jobs on his/her probability of employment may be very different depending on personal circumstances. It is, therefore, important to investigate the job access effect separately for different groups. This chapter provides estimates of the importance of job access to youth employment for the following groups: black, white, and Hispanic youths; youths living in different sized

59

metropolitan areas; youths living in central city and suburban areas; youths living in families with different incomes; and youths attending and not attending school. The six specific questions I attempt to answer with the data are listed below.

1. Is the substantial amount of the racial difference in youth employment rates that can be attributed to differential job access found in our earlier work for Philadelphia a unique result?[1] Reinforcing this concern is the fact that the Philadelphia housing market is more highly segregated along racial lines than markets in most other metropolitan areas.[2] Ideally, separate analyses of a large number of different metropolitan areas that replicate the methodology we used for Philadelphia would be conducted. Unfortunately, this is precluded by the limitations of the available data. As a second best solution, I estimate job probability equations, which include an intrametropolitan measure of job access using random samples of youths drawn from 50 different metropolitan areas.

2. The empirical literature on the spatial mismatch hypothesis has focused on black joblessness, with little attention having been paid to the employment problems of Hispanics. The employment rates of Hispanic youths, while higher than those observed for black teenagers, are low relative to the employment rates of white youths. To what extent is this gap attributable to differences in intraurban job accessibility?

3. The income level of a youth's family may affect all three of the relevant variables, namely, reservation wage, unit transportation costs, and job information, that determine the magnitude of the job access effect. The youth's reservation wage and his/her family income are known to be directly related (Holzer 1986). Transportation costs may be lower for youths from higher income families because of easier access to automobile transportation. The youth's acquisition of word-of-mouth information on available jobs may be better or worse in families with higher incomes. On the one hand, parents who earn higher salaries may have more extensive business and social contacts to draw upon in helping their children find suitable jobs. On the other hand, parents of lower socioeconomic status might know more about the types of jobs youths are qualified to hold, since they are more likely to work in one of

the youth-intensive occupational categories (i.e., sales, clerical, service, and labor).

If poor job access does reduce the job probability for teenagers from lower income families, this may help to explain the strong tendency for youth employment to rise with the level of family income within racial groups. To what extent, then, is the employment rate gap between youths from low- and high-income families within the same racial group attributable to differences in job access?

4. The spatial mismatch hypothesis has been put forward as a possible explanation for the employment problems experienced by blacks living in the central cities of large metropolitan areas. However, large differences in employment rates between white and black youths exist in both large and small metropolitan areas. Does the importance of job access as an explanation for the racial difference in youth employment rates differ depending on the population size of the metropolitan area?

5. Employment rates for youths of all races are lower in larger, as compared to smaller, metropolitan areas. How much of this difference can be attributed to the possibility that youths in smaller areas may possess superior access to jobs?

6. Finally, Wilson (1987) has suggested that the effect of job access on the black youth's job probability may differ between the central city and the suburban ring. He decries the absence of job networks in the central city poverty neighborhoods where young blacks reside: "Even in those situations where job vacancies become available in an industry near or within an inner-city neighborhood, workers who live outside the inner city may find out about these vacancies sooner than those who live near the industry because the latter are not tied into the job network" (p. 60).[3] According to Wilson, these networks have failed to develop in the inner city because the people are socially isolated, which he defines as lacking contact or sustained interaction with individuals and institutions that represent mainstream society. Thus, central city blacks lack access to jobs due to their social rather than geographical distance.

In addition to predicting a weaker relationship between job proximity and employment for central city versus suburban black youths, Wilson's depiction of central city poverty neighborhoods implies that a black teenager's probability of having a job will be lower in central cities in comparison to suburban areas, even after controlling for the youth's individual and family characteristics. He has argued that the outmigration of upwardly mobile blacks has left fewer and weaker institutional supports, such as churches and schools, and fewer middle- or working-class role models for the central city poor, causing negative changes in the employment and labor force behaviors of those who have been left behind. Wilson has termed the influence of neighborhood characteristics on individual behavior as "concentration effects." The interesting questions suggested by Wilson's work are how much of the lower employment rates observed for central city, in comparison to suburban, black youths can be attributed to the presence of concentration effects within central cities, and how much of this difference is due to central city black teenagers living farther from jobs than their suburban counterparts?

Data Collection and Empirical Methodology

The basic estimating equation used to investigate the six questions listed in the previous section can be expressed as:

$$P_i(E)=f(T_i,I_i,F_i,M_i), \tag{3.1}$$

where $P_i(E)$ is the probability that the ith *youth is employed, and the* T_i, I_i, F_i, and M_i are commuting time, the individual's characteristics, the characteristics of the youth's family, and a set of metropolitan area dummy variables, respectively. Each of the independent variables is described below.

The measure of job access (T_i) is the average one-way commuting time to work by low-wage workers (wage rate $\leq$ \$5.00 per hour) who travel by private, motorized carrier (i.e., automobile, truck, or motorcycle) and who live in the same residential zone as the youths.[4] To capture both intrazonal and interzonal differences in job access among racial groups, separate mean travel times for each zone are computed for white, black, and Hispanic workers.[5]

T_i was chosen as the measure of job access for a number of reasons. First, Ellwood's (1986) experimentation, as well as my own with alternative measures, revealed that travel time is the strongest predictor of job probability. Other measures tried are the proportion of all jobs in the SMSA that can be reached within 30 minutes of the residential zone by public transit and the ratio of jobs located in the zone to the number of workers residing in the zone.

Ellwood experimented with both of these measures, while my own experimentation was restricted by the data to variously defined ratios of jobs to workers (e.g., all jobs to all workers, low-wage jobs to low-wage workers, etc.).[6] Second, T_i is the identical measure of job access that we employed in our Philadelphia study, which facilitates comparisons with our earlier work. Finally, except for the possible use of actual travel distances, which are not provided by the data, travel time is conceptually the most meaningful measure of job access, since it reflects actual worker behavior. If jobs are nearby, commuting time will be low. Conversely, if jobs cannot be found nearby, travel time will be high.

The restrictions placed on the sample of workers used to compute mean travel time—namely, only automobile travelers who earn a low wage—are intended to control for differences in the mix of transportation modes across zones and to define the job opportunity set most applicable to youths.[7] All low-wage workers, rather than just young workers, are used to compute times, because in many zones too few youth observations are available to compute a reliable estimate of expected commuting time. In addition, youth travel times in zones with poor job access may underestimate the required commute of the marginal teenager interested in obtaining a job, if working youths, as compared to adult workers, are less able or less willing to commute to more distant jobs.[8]

The individual and family variables defined in table 3.1 are those employed in our earlier work. They were originally selected to conform as closely as the data allowed to the variables found in prior studies of youth employment (Freeman 1982; Ehrenberg and Marcus 1982). Their means and standard deviations, broken down by race and enrollment status, are provided in the appendix to this chapter. The metro-

Table 3.1   Definitions of Individual and Family Variables

Personal Characteristics

Age of youth in years

Years of school completed

Spouse of youth present in household (Yes=1)

Youth has no mental or physical problems limiting the type of work
   (Yes=1)

Youth is a female (Yes=1)

Youth is a high school graduate (Yes=1)

Youth has borne a child (Yes=1)

Family Background

Residence in one-parent—female-headed family (Yes=1)

Completed years of education of head of household

Other family income (reference category=less than $10,000)

Annual family income net of youth's earnings greater than $10,000 and
   less than $20,000 (Yes=1)

Net family income between $20,000 and $30,000 (Yes=1)

Net family income between $30,000 and $40,000 (Yes=1)

Net family income greater than $40,000 (Yes=1)

Occupation of household head (reference category=head without a job)

Manager or professional (Yes=1)

Technical, sales, or administrative support (Yes=1)

Service (Yes=1)

Precision production, craft or repair (Yes=1)

Operator, fabricator, or laborer (Yes=1)

---

politan area dummy variables control for supply and demand factors that differ across metropolitan areas and may affect the probability of youths having a job.[9]

The data come from the 1980 Public-Use Samples. Two different youth samples were taken from the 50 SMSAs for which the sample identifies at least four residential zones per metropolitan area. (See the appendix to this chapter for the list of SMSAs used.)[10] Sample 1 is completely random; therefore, the percentage of observations in the sample from a particular SMSA reflects its relative population size. To form sample 2, the 50 SMSAs were divided into four groups of 13 or 12 members, based on the population size of the metropolitan area, and random samples of approximately the same size were taken from each group.

The group of largest SMSAs had a minimum population of 2.3 million. SMSAs in the second group had populations larger than 1.4 million but smaller than 2.3 million. The third group consisted of SMSAs of between 1.4 million and 0.8 million people. The group of smallest SMSAs had populations of fewer than 0.8 million people. While four was the minimum number of residential zones qualifying the SMSA for selection into the sample, 35 of the SMSAs had five or more zones, and 14 had at least 10 zones. The mean number of zones was eight.[11]

Since I had no *a priori* expectation regarding the appropriate functional form to use to estimate the job probability equations, both dichotomous logit and linear probability function models were estimated. Although logit is the more common approach, Stoker (1986) has shown that ordinary least squares may be more appropriate in a broad variety of circumstances. In most cases, the results obtained with the linear probability model and the logit model were highly similar.[12] Except where noted, the tables in the text of this chapter are, therefore, based on only the logit results. Complete results are provided in the appendix to this chapter.

Overall Sample Results

Based on sample 1, separate estimates of the effect of intraurban job accessibility on the probability of having a job were obtained for the following four groups of youth: (1) 16 to 19-year-olds, living at home, and enrolled in school; (2) 16 to 19-year-olds, living at home, and not enrolled in school; (3) 20 to 24-year-olds, living at home, not enrolled in school, and having less than a college education; (4) 20 to 24-year-olds, not living at home, neither enrolled in school nor in the military, and having less than a college education.[13]

The full set of individual and family variables enter the equations estimated for teenagers. Because family background information is not available for youths no longer living at home, a subset of the independent variables are used for the older, not-at-home youth: age, years of school, high school diploma, sex, health status, income net of the youth's earnings, marital status, and whether the person has ever borne a child. For consistency, these same variables entered the equations estimated for the older at-home group.

Focusing first on the results obtained for enrolled teenagers, the first column of table 3.2 gives the estimated increase in job probability that would result from a five-minute reduction in travel time. Five minutes is used as the hypothetical improvement in job access because, from a policy perspective, it is a savings in travel time of a reasonable amount. In addition, five minutes is roughly a one standard deviation change in time for blacks and Hispanics and a two standard deviation time change for whites. Regardless of race, the effect of better job access is found to be substantial, ranging from a 5.5 percentage point increase in the job probability of blacks and Hispanics to a 7.0 percentage point increase for whites.

All of the estimates are statistically significant at a very high level. The strength of the job access effects can be further illustrated by estimating the *percentage* change in the employment rate of each group from the hypothetical improvement in job access. Calculated at the mean employment rate for each group, a five-minute reduction in travel time would cause a 17 percent increase in the employment rate of whites, a 29 percent increase in the employment rate of blacks, and a 19 percent increase in the employment rate of Hispanics. Clearly, job access has a highly significant economic effect on the employment of enrolled teenagers, regardless of racial group.

Among enrolled youths, blacks and Hispanics have higher mean travel times than whites, and these differences are statistically significant at the 1 percent level by a two-tailed test (table 3.2, column 3). A portion of the difference in employment rates between whites and the other two racial groups can therefore be attributed to differential job access. To determine the magnitude of this portion for blacks, the probability of having a job was predicted for a black youth with black

Table 3.2 Results for the Overall Sample of Youths Living in 50 SMSAs

	Change in Job Probability Due to a Five-Minute Decrease in Travel Time	t-Statistic	Mean Travel Time (Minutes)	Employment Rate	Percentage Change in Employment Rate Gap from:		Sample Size
					Substitution of White Time for Minority Time	Substitution of White Effect for Minority Effect	
16–19 Years Old Enrolled							
Whites	.070	4.54	18.70	.418			8,500
Blacks	.055	6.04	24.20	.190	−27	32[a]	9,400
Hispanics	.055	4.71	22.75	.292	−35	0	7,313
16–19 Years Old Not Enrolled							
Whites	.030	1.10	18.58	.691			2,492
Blacks	.065	3.48	24.40	.338	−21	−48	3,296
Hispanics	.035	1.53	22.60	.480	−13	−11[a]	3,234
20–24 Years Old At Home							
Whites	.040	2.35	18.80	.786			4,235
Blacks	.055	3.67	24.40	.508	−22	−26[a]	5,908
Hispanics	.045	2.60	22.86	.658	−26	−16[a]	4,488
20–24 Years Old Not at Home							
Whites	.015	1.09	18.66	.747			6,464
Blacks	.050	3.13	23.70	.576	−29	−97	5,540
Hispanics	.035	2.29	22.41	.627	−22	−75[a]	7,161

[a] Indicates that the minority group estimated effect is not significantly different from the estimated effect for white youth at the 10 percent level by a two-tailed test.

mean values of all characteristics, represented by $\overline{X}$, but with the same accessibility to jobs as the average white youth:

$$\hat{P}_B=\hat{a}_B+\hat{b}_B\overline{X}_B+\hat{c}_B\overline{T}_W,\tag{3.2}$$

where W and B refer to the white and black samples, respectively. The difference between $\hat{P}_B$ and the actual employment rate for white youths yields an estimate of the hypothetical racial difference in employment rates that would exist if blacks and whites had identical job access. To obtain the percentage of the employment rate difference between whites and blacks that can be attributed to differential job access, the hypothetical difference in employment rates is subtracted from the actual difference in employment rates, and expressed as a percentage of the actual difference.

Twenty-seven percent of the gap in employment rates between white and black enrolled teenagers can be attributed to the inferior job access suffered by blacks (see table 3.2, column 5). Of the white-Hispanic employment rate difference, 35 percent is due to a job access differential. These numbers indicate that while job access does not account for the entirety of the existing racial gaps in youth employment rates, it certainly plays an important role in understanding these differences.

It is also of interest to determine how racial differences in employment rates would change if the effect of travel time on job probability were the same for minorities as for whites. To determine this for blacks, the probability of having a job was predicted using the following equation:

$$\hat{P}_B=\hat{a}_B+\hat{b}_B\overline{X}_B+\hat{c}_W\overline{T}_B.\tag{3.3}$$

This equation predicts what the employment rate of average black youths would be if they were affected by job access in the same manner as whites. Following the same methodology outlined above for computing the portion of the employment rate difference attributable to differences in job access, equation (3.3) was used to estimate the change in the racial employment rate difference if blacks were affected by job access in the same manner as whites (see table 3.2, column 6). As it turns out, these estimates are not particularly interesting in the case of enrolled teenagers, since differences in the effects of travel time are small across groups and are not statistically significant. As noted below, this will not always be true for the other groups.

Turning now to the results obtained for teenage youths who are not in school, estimates suggest that the job access effect varies among the racial groups. For white and Hispanic teenagers, the effects are small relative to those observed for enrolled youths. These results suggest that in comparison to their enrolled counterparts, white and Hispanic teenagers who are not in school are less affected by job access in their quest for employment. This is not true for blacks, however. In their case, the job access effect is somewhat larger for nonenrolled youths when compared to those who are enrolled. At the mean employment rate for nonenrolled blacks, the results indicate that a five-minute reduction in travel time would increase their probability of having a job by about 20 percent.

In the case of nonenrolled youths, travel time differences between whites and the two minority groups are again statistically significant. These differences in job access explain 21 percent and 13 percent of the black-white and Hispanic-white gaps in employment rates, respectively. Since estimated black and white job access effects are significantly different, it is also of interest to determine how the racial gap in employment rates would change if blacks were affected by job access in the same manner as whites. If this were true, the employment rate difference between black and white nonenrolled youths would be reduced by almost one-half according to my results.

Although my analysis focuses on teenagers, I also estimated the importance of job access to youths aged 20 to 24, since racial differences in employment rates are also large for young adults. For those youths still living at home, the estimated effects of job access are similar in magnitude, and are not statistically different, among the racial groups. The magnitude of the effects, which are all statistically significant, are somewhat smaller than those observed for teenagers in school. The percentage of the white-minority employment rate difference that can be attributed to differentials in job access is 29 and 22 percent for blacks and Hispanics, respectively.

Finally, there are the results obtained for older youths who are not living at home. As noted in chapter 2, these results may suffer from biases resulting from possible simultaneity between employment status and residential location. However, the problem is expected to be less severe in the case of minority youth, since their choice of location is constrained by housing market discrimination.

As the simultaneity problem might lead us to expect, the effect of job access on the employment of white youth not living at home is not significantly different from zero. However, for Hispanics and blacks, an improvement in job access increases the probability of having a job by about the same magnitudes as those observed for youth still living at home. The results suggest that 29 percent of the difference between the white and black employment rates can be attributed to differential job access of the white/Hispanic employment rate gap, 22 percent is due to a job access differential. It is also of interest to note that if blacks were affected by job access in the same manner as whites, black and white employment rates would be essentially the same.

The results obtained for the overall sample indicate that job access has an important effect on the job probabilities of both teenagers and young adults and that racial differences in job access are important in understanding the relatively high level of joblessness among black and Hispanic youths. The estimated effects of travel time on the probability that a youth has a job, however, are smaller than the ones we obtained in our Philadelphia study. One possible explanation was our ability to better measure job access for Philadelphia black and white youths, since 26 residential zones for this area are identified by the 1980 Public-Use Sample. The smaller the residential zone in geographic area, the better the estimate of expected commuting time, assuming a sufficient number of worker observations are available to compute a reliable average. In recognition of this, I re-estimated the equations for teenagers, restricting the sample to those living in the 14 SMSAs for which at least 10 residential zones are identified. Black and white results are presented in table 3.3. For comparison purposes, this table also includes the results obtained for the full sample, along with the estimates for Philadelphia.

There is little difference for whites or blacks in the magnitudes of the

**Table 3.3   The Effect of a Five-Minute Reduction in Travel Time
on the Job Probability of Teenagers:
A Comparison of Results from Different Samples**

	Philadelphia Sample	Sample of 50 SMSAs	Sample of 14 SMSAs
Enrolled			
Whites	.085	.070	.065
	(7.87)[a]	(4.54)	(3.36)
Blacks	.055	.055	.060
	(3.17)	(6.04)	(6.09)
Not Enrolled			
Whites	.100	.030	.025
	(4.92)	(1.10)	(0.49)
Blacks	.085	.065	.065
	(4.61)	(3.48)	(3.48)

[a] t-statistics indicating whether the estimated job access effect is significantly different from zero are in parentheses.

job access effects between the 50-SMSA and 14-SMSA samples. This is a reassuring result, since it suggests that measurement error in the travel time variable is not an important concern. The estimated job access effects for blacks who are in school are essentially the same across all three samples. For blacks who are not in school, the Philadelphia estimate is somewhat larger than the other two. For whites, the Philadelphia estimates are larger than those obtained with the other two samples, especially in the case of nonenrolled youths. These results suggest that either (1) the job probabilities of Philadelphia white youths are more strongly affected by job access than are those of white youths living in other metropolitan areas, or (2) job access is better measured for white youths in Philadelphia than for youths in other metropolitan areas. In light of the similarity in the results for whites between the 14-SMSA and 50-SMSA samples and the similarity in the results for blacks between the 14-SMSA and the Philadelphia samples, I am more inclined to believe the first proposal rather than the second, although I can offer no convincing explanation as to why the job access effect is stronger for Philadelphia white youths.

Using the same decomposition technique embodied in equation (3.2), the results from our Philadelphia study suggested that about 35 percent of the employment rate difference between black and white teenagers could be attributed to differential access to jobs. This is higher than the portions suggested by the results obtained with the 50-SMSA sample. Since the estimated effect of job access on black employment is very similar between these two samples, the results must vary because job access differences between blacks and whites are larger for Philadelphia than for the 50-SMSA sample. The racial difference in travel time for enrolled teenagers, for example, is 7.43 minutes in Philadelphia, but only 5.50 minutes for youths in the 50-SMSA sample. Other large cities also have large variances in travel time between blacks and whites; for example, the racial time difference in New York and Chicago is larger than in Philadelphia.[14] Our Philadelphia results, therefore, probably do not overstate the importance of job access in explaining racial differences in youth employment in very large metropolitan areas.

In summary, the results indicate that our earlier conclusions based on Philadelphia data are correct; namely, that job access has an important effect on whether a youth has a job and that differential job access between the races is important to our understanding of the black-white difference in youth employment rates. In addition, there are two other important findings. First, the inferior job access of Hispanic youths is an important reason for their lower employment rates relative to whites. This is particularly true for enrolled youths, where 35 percent of the white-Hispanic employment rate difference can be attributed to differential job access. Overall, the role of job access is roughly of the same importance in explaining the relatively low employment rates of both Hispanics and blacks. Second, for some groups of black youths, namely, teenagers not in school and older youth not living at home, the evidence suggests that their relatively low employment rates are not only the result of poor job access, but are due also to a stronger effect of job access on job probability. Explanations for this finding include the possibility that these youths have greater difficulty commuting to distant jobs—perhaps because automobile transportation is not available—or have less information about more distant job openings—perhaps because of poor informal job networks.

Results for Youths with Different Family Incomes

As discussed in the first section of this chapter, there are reasons to believe that the magnitude of the job access effect on youth employment will be larger for youths from families with lower incomes. There are other equally plausible reasons, however, to believe just the opposite, namely that youths with higher family income will be impacted the most. The issue, therefore, can only be settled empirically. In this section, I present results that shed light on the extent to which (1) the strength of the job access effect on youth job probability varies with family income, and (2) the differences in youth employment rates between high- and low-income families within the same racial group can be attributed to differences in job access. As documented in table 3.4, in all three racial groups youth employment rates rise precipitously with the level of family income.

To investigate whether the magnitude of the job access effect varies with family income, job probability equations were estimated that included the same set of variables described earlier, plus the interaction of travel time with a set of dummy variables representing the income categories listed in table 3.4.[15] These results were used to construct table 3.5, which shows the estimated increase in job probability due to a five-minute reduction in travel time for youths in each of the family income categories, broken down by race and enrollment status. The magnitudes of the job access effects are remarkably similar across income categories. In addition, for each race/enrollment group, the results are consistent with earlier conclusions that were based on the results obtained from the overall sample; namely, that job access has an important effect on the job probabilities of all groups of teenagers, except whites and Hispanics not enrolled in school. The results for nonenrolled Hispanics, however, do indicate that the job access effect is

Table 3.4 Employment Rates and Travel Times for Teenagers with Different Family Incomes

| | Blacks | | | | Hispanics | | | | Whites | | | |
| | Enrolled | | Not Enrolled | | Enrolled | | Not Enrolled | | Enrolled | | Not Enrolled | |
	Emp. Rate	Mean Time	Emp. Rate	Mean Time	Emp. Rate	Mean Time	Emp. Rate	Mean Time	Emp. Rate	Mean Time	Emp. Rate	Mean Time
$Y \leq \$10,000$	.151	24.4	.268	24.7	.211	24.9	.366	24.3	.296	19.0	.575	18.9
$\$10,000 < Y \leq \$20,000$	.183	24.4	.354	24.4	.281	23.0	.481	22.4	.409	18.7	.609	18.8
$\$20,000 < Y \leq \$30,000$	.212	23.9	.402	24.1	.321	21.8	.528	21.7	.430	18.6	.724	18.8
$\$30,000 < Y \leq \$40,000$	.232	23.8	.427	23.7	.380	21.2	.624	20.8	.455	18.6	.755	18.7
$Y > \$40,000$	.231	23.4	.439	23.5	.354	20.9	.678	21.0	.415	18.6	.753	18.6

important for youths from low-income families. Overall, the evidence indicates that for most youths job access has a strong and fairly uniform effect on the probability of having a job, regardless of the level of family income.

Since travel times systematically decline as family income rises (see table 3.4), a portion of the difference in employment rates between youths from low- and high-income families can be attributed to job access. To determine the size of this portion, I used the methodology described earlier, with appropriate modifications, to predict the job probability of low-income youth (annual family income net of the youth's earnings less than $10,000) under the assumption that they have the same access to jobs as high-income youth (annual family income greater than $40,000). The percentages of the employment rate difference between youths in low- and high-income families attributable to job access are reported at the bottom of table 3.5. These percentages for enrolled and nonenrolled teenagers are modest in size for blacks (13 percent and 8 percent) and Hispanics (25 percent and 12 percent), but are small in magnitude for whites (4 percent and 1 percent).

The differences in travel time across income categories capture only interzonal differences in job access. It may be the case that because of income segregation in housing patterns within zones, youths from lower income families have longer expected commuting times than youth from higher income families who live within the same residential zone. The travel time differences among income categories reported in table 3.4 would therefore understate true differences in job access. To investigate this, I took a random sample of 10 SMSAs from the 50-SMSA sample and computed for each family income category—separately for blacks and whites—the average travel time across all zones of workers who satisfied the same restrictions placed on the sample used to compute the travel times that serve as the measure of job access, namely, low-wage workers who travelled to work by private, motorized carrier. Differences in these averages across income categories reflect both inter-and intrazonal variation in job accessibility.

As reported in table 3.6, for nine of the SMSAs in the case of whites and six of the SMSAs in the case of blacks, average travel times do

Table 3.5 The Effect of a Five-Minute Reduction in Travel Time on the Job Probability of Teenagers with Different Family Incomes

	Blacks		Hispanics		Whites	
	Enrolled	Not Enrolled	Enrolled	Not Enrolled	Enrolled	Not Enrolled
$Y \leq \$10,000$	.045	.055	.045	.055	.060	.010
	(4.11)[a]	(2.55)	(3.53)	(2.38)	(1.84)	(0.20)
$\$10,000 < Y \leq \$20,000$	.045	.055	.045	.005	.080	.025
	(0.34)	(0.10)	(0.20)	(2.34)	(0.55)	(0.23)
$\$20,000 < Y \leq \$30,000$	.045	.080	.030	.050	.050	.050
	(0.30)	(0.94)	(1.11)	(0.05)	(0.22)	(0.72)
$\$30,000 < Y \leq \$40,000$	.065	.055	.045	.005	.055	.005
	(1.31)	(0.04)	(0.03)	(1.54)	(0.17)	(0.08)
$Y > \$40,000$	.060	.060	.050	.015	.050	.035
	(0.92)	(0.14)	(0.24)	(1.76)	(0.25)	(0.36)
Amount of the high/ low income employment rate gap due to job access	13%	8%	25%	12%	4%	1%

[a] The first row of numbers in parentheses are t-statistics that indicate the statistical significance of travel time for youth from families with incomes of less than $10,000. The other numbers in parentheses are t-statistics that indicate whether the travel-time effect is significantly different between the higher income groups and the low-income group.

Table 3.6 Mean Travel Times for Selected Metropolitan Areas

	Chicago		Dayton		Indianapolis		Tampa		Milwaukee	
	Whites	Blacks	Whites	Blacks	Whites	Blacks	Whites	Blacks	Whites	Blacks
$Y < \$10,000$	20.9	29.1	17.0	18.8	18.4	20.0	18.7	20.2	16.3	20.1
$\$10,000 < Y \leq \$20,000$	19.9	28.7	17.2	19.5	18.1	19.8	18.5	20.0	16.2	21.3
$\$20,000 < Y \leq \$30,000$	18.7	27.5	16.1	19.5	17.2	20.8	18.4	21.6	15.1	16.6
$\$30,000 < Y \leq \$40,000$	17.4	28.4	15.0	18.9	17.6	20.0	17.9	20.7	15.0	16.5
$Y > \$40,000$	17.8	26.7	16.1	22.1	17.6	21.3	17.2	19.0	14.4	16.0

	Dallas		Greensboro		Norfolk		New Orleans		Pittsburgh	
	Whites	Blacks	Whites	Blacks	Whites	Blacks	Whites	Blacks	Whites	Blacks
$Y < \$10,000$	19.0	21.9	15.8	16.5	19.0	20.5	20.6	23.7	18.9	20.4
$\$10,000 < Y \leq \$20,000$	19.6	24.2	16.9	17.4	19.8	22.7	21.0	22.8	17.9	22.9
$\$20,000 < Y \leq \$30,000$	19.2	22.9	16.7	17.2	19.6	22.3	18.9	24.5	17.6	19.7
$\$30,000 < Y \leq \$40,000$	18.9	21.4	15.7	16.7	19.3	22.1	19.1	23.3	17.6	20.3
$Y > \$40,000$	18.2	21.8	15.1	12.5	19.6	24.9	18.4	19.0	17.2	22.9

decline with family income level. In all cases, however, the differences in times between the lowest and highest income categories are small and similar in magnitude to the differences based on only interzonal variation. These results suggest that the importance of job access as an explanatory factor for differences in employment rates between youths with high and low family incomes — within the same racial category — is not understated by the percentages reported in table 3.5.

To summarize the results presented in this section, there are three important findings. First, job access is an important determinant of the employment probabilities of enrolled teenagers at all levels of family income. This holds true for all three racial groups. Second, for teenagers not in school, the job access effect is uniformly strong at all family income levels for blacks and uniformly weak at all family income levels for whites. The job access effect varies in strength with family income level for nonenrolled Hispanics, with the effect found to be much stronger for youth with lower family incomes. Third, because differences in the distance to jobs between youths from low- and high-income families tend to be small within the same racial group, job access plays only a modest role, at best, in explaining differences in youth employment rates at different family income levels.

Results for Youth Living in Different Sized Metropolitan Areas

In this section, the job access effects estimated for teenage youth living in the four different sized classes of metropolitan areas that form sample 2 are discussed (see table 3.7). These estimates were obtained by estimating separate job-probability equations for each class of metropolitan areas. The equations contain the same independent variables as before.

For enrolled youths, the estimated effects of job access tend to be similar among the three largest sized classes of metropolitan areas. These estimates are roughly of the same magnitude as those obtained with sample 1. In other words, job access is found to have a strong effect on a youth's job probability as long as he/she lives in a metropolitan area with more than 800,000 people. However, for youth living in the smallest sized class of metropolitan areas (i.e., fewer than 800,000 in population), none of the job access effects for any of the racial groups is significantly different from zero. Job access effects are found to be important for out-of-school youths if they live in the largest sized class of metropolitan areas in the case of whites and Hispanics, or in the two largest sized classes in the case of blacks. For Hispanics, the tendency for estimated job access effects to be statistically insignificant for smaller metropolitan areas may reflect the fact that sample sizes are relatively small; however, this is not a problem for the other two racial groups. For them, the results suggest that the effect of job access on the probability that the youth has a job is stronger within larger metropolitan areas, especially for nonenrolled youths. It is also possible, however, that measurement error in the job access variable accounts for these results.

As previously discussed, the mean travel time of residential zones containing large land areas is expected to be a less reliable indicator of a youth's true access to jobs. Since the geographic size of the average residential zone increases as the size of the metropolitan area declines, there may be greater measurement error in the job access variable for smaller metropolitan areas. Measurement error in an independent variable typically causes the true effect of the variable to be underestimated. Allaying this concern somewhat is the fact that the results reported in table 3.3 for the 50-SMSA and the 14-SMSA samples were virtually indistinguishable. This evidence does not rule out the possibility that measurement error explains, at least in part, the smaller job access effects observed for smaller metropolitan areas.

As it turns out, the measurement error issue is largely rendered mute by the small differences in travel times that exist between races within smaller metropolitan areas. For example, in the smallest sized class of metropolitan areas, where the job access effect is consistently small and statistically insignificant, travel time difference between blacks and whites is only 1.4 minutes. Even if youths in small areas were affected by job access in the same manner as youth in large areas, differential job

Table 3.7 Results for Teenagers Living in Different Sized Metropolitan Areas

| | Change in Job Probability Due to a Five-Minute Decrease in Travel Time | t-Statistic | Mean Travel Time (Minutes) | Employment Rate | Percentage Change in Employment Rate Gap from: | | Sample Size |
					Substitution of White Time for Minority Time	Substitution of White Effect for Minority Effect[a]	
Enrolled							
Whites							
S1[b]	.040	1.43	16.37	.390			3,654
S2	.075	2.60	17.86	.451			4,459
S3	.090	2.77	18.37	.430			4,413
S4	.055	3.22	19.48	.421			4,862
Blacks							
S1	.025	0.75	17.78	.176	−3	17[c]	2,000
S2	.050	1.66	21.06	.227	−14	47[c]	4,209
S3	.065	4.54	23.03	.202	−27	50[c]	7,061
S4	.040	4.43	25.85	.175	−21	31[c]	5,009
Hispanics							
S1	.015	0.41	16.37	.263	0	64[c]	410
S2	.015	0.22	18.26	.372	−2	277	1,037
S3	.045	2.04	20.53	.376	−36	342[c]	2,813
S4	.055	6.16	25.00	.245	−35	0[c]	8,286

Not Enrolled							
Whites							
S1	.045	1.78	16.37	.670			4,350
S2	.010	0.50	17.89	.681			6,759
S3	−.020	0.70	18.57	.694			4,706
S4	.055	3.38	19.59	.677			4,590
Blacks							
S1	.015	0.84	17.73	.,357	−1	33[c]	495
S2	−.035	0.69	26.01	.377	7	62[c]	1,602
S3	.115	3.85	23.37	.327	−30	−172	2,688
S4	.060	5.26	26.11	.327	−22	−7[c]	6,505
Hispanics							
S1	.020	0.25	16.48	.480	0	43[c]	172
S2	.015	0.10	18.14	.524	0	−11[c]	426
S3	−.005	0.33	20.00	.546	0	−40[c]	1,174
S4	.055	3.15	24.70	.452	−25	0	3,688

[a] Estimates in excess of 100 percent indicate that the employment rate of the minority group would rise above that of whites if the white effect were substituted for the minority effect.

[b] S1 represents SMSAs with populations of fewer than 0.8 million, S2 are SMSAs between 0.8 and 1.4 million in population; S3 are SMSAs larger than 1.4 million but smaller than 2.3 million; and S4 are SMSAs with more than 2.3 million people.

[c] Indicates that the minority group job access effect is not significantly different from the effect estimated for white youth at the 10 percent level by a two-tailed test.

access would play a relatively unimportant role in explaining the racial gap in youth employment rates.

In the two largest sized classes of metropolitan areas, racial differences in travel time are substantial. For example, for metropolitan areas with more than 2.3 million people, the black time is 33 percent greater than the white time. Job access differentials are therefore important in explaining the relatively low employment rates of blacks and Hispanics living within larger metropolitan areas. For blacks, 21 to 30 percent of the black/white employment rate gap can be attributed to racial differences in job access, depending on the group considered. The corresponding range for Hispanics is from 25 to 35 percent.

In summary, two important conclusions can be drawn from the results obtained for the different sized metropolitan areas. First, for all three racial groups, regardless of enrollment status, job access is found to have a strong effect on the employment of youths living in metropolitan areas with more than 2.3 million people. For these youths the job access effect is remarkably robust. Second, the results for teenagers, both in and out of school, suggest that the importance of job access as an explanation for racial differences in employment rates is considerably greater in larger, as compared to smaller, metropolitan areas. The principal reason for this is that in smaller metropolitan areas youths tend to have good job access regardless of where they reside, so racial differences in accessibility tend to be small in magnitude. In addition, the results suggest that the effect of job access on the probability of being employed may be weaker in smaller metropolitan areas, especially for those not enrolled in school.

The other issue that can be addressed using the results obtained from estimating job probability equations for youths living in different sized metropolitan areas is the extent to which job access explains the tendency for employment rates to decline as the population of the area increases. As shown in table 3.7 (column 4), employment rates are highest for those who live in metropolitan areas in the second smallest sized class and are the lowest for those who live in the largest metropolitan areas. This is true for youths who are in or out of school, for all three racial groups. Table 3.8 reports the estimated portion of the

Table 3.8   Estimated Percentage Change in the Employment Rate Difference Between Large and Small Metropolitan Areas if Youths Had the Same Access to Jobs

Whites	
Enrolled	−59
Not Enrolled	−467[a]
Blacks	
Enrolled	−74
Not Enrolled	−122
Hispanics	
Enrolled	−58
Not Enrolled	−100

NOTE: Estimates were obtained by substituting the mean travel time of small metropolitan areas for the mean travel time of large metropolitan areas.

[a] Estimates in excess of 100 percent indicate that the employment rate in large metropolitan areas would rise above the employment rate in small metropolitan areas if youth had the same access to jobs.

employment rate difference between the class sizes of metropolitan areas that can be attributed to differences in the access to jobs. For each of the racial/enrollment groups, large portions of the difference in employment rates between large and small areas can be attributed to youths in smaller areas having better access to jobs. In fact, for those not enrolled in school, equalizing job access would cause employment rates in large metropolitan areas to be equal to or greater than those prevailing within small areas.

Results for Youths Living in Central City and Suburban Areas

In this section, the focus of the analysis is on the two hypotheses advanced by Wilson (1987) concerning the high rate of joblessness among out-of-school black youths living in large central cities. As reported in table 3.9, the employment rate of these youths is much lower than that of the other nonenrolled groups (i.e., suburban blacks and whites and Hispanics, regardless of location). To reiterate Wilson's hypotheses, he has suggested that (1) job access has little effect on the employment of central city black youths, because they are isolated both socially and economically from mainstream society, and (2) a considerable portion of the high level of black youth joblessness can be attributed to the existence of concentration effects within central city neighborhoods.

Table 3.9 also reveals that employment rates are lower for youths of all three racial groups living in central cities in comparison to their suburban counterparts, regardless of enrollment status. Another objective of this section is, therefore, to determine the extent to which job access explains employment rate differentials between central city and suburban areas.

Since Wilson's hypotheses refer to youths living in large central cities, the observations used to estimate separate job-probability equations for central city and suburban youths come from the largest 25 metropolitan areas represented in our 50-SMSA sample. Recall that these areas have 1980 populations exceeding 1.4 million. The control variables include the set of individual and family variables described earlier, but exclude the metropolitan area dummy variables. The use of these variables is problematic when stratifying the sample into central city and suburban areas, since for each racial group there is only one travel time mean for each central city.

As an alternative approach, a set of five variables is included. They describe those aspects of each metropolitan area that theory suggests may affect youth employment: (1) the metropolitan area unemployment rate; (2) the fraction of the metropolitan area labor force who are women over the age of 19 who have a high school education or less; (3) the fraction of the metropolitan areas jobs available in youth-intensive occupations (i.e., service workers, laborers, operatives, sales workers, and clerical workers), (4) the fraction of the metropolitan area population who are black, and (5) the population of the metropolitan area.

The unemployment rate measures the overall tightness of the metropolitan labor market. Less-educated adult women as a percentage of the labor force is included, since the work of Osterman (1980), Grant and Hamermesh (1981), and Borjas (1986) suggests that adult females may

Table 3.9 Results for Teenagers Living Within Central City and Suburban Areas

| | Change in Job Probability Due to a Five-Minute Decrease in Travel Time | t-Statistic | Mean Travel Time (Minutes) | Employment Rate | Percentage Change in Employment Rate Gap from:[a] | | Sample Size |
					Substitution of Suburban Time for City Time[b]	Substitution of Suburban Effect for City Effect[b]	
Enrolled							
Whites							
Central City	.075	1.58	20.84	.402			1,619
Suburbs	.055	3.08	18.57	.430	−121	−297[b]	7,436
Blacks							
Central City	.065	4.48	25.60	.183			7,784
Suburbs	.055	4.05	21.72	.205	−229	−233[b]	3,802
Hispanics							
Central City	.100	6.20	26.87	.210			6,116
Suburbs	.030	1.53	20.93	.369	−75	−236	2,849
Not Enrolled							
Whites							
Central City	.035	.75	20.71	.606			1,936
Suburbs	.040	2.04	18.67	.706	−14	21[b]	7,111
Blacks							
Central City	.075	3.56	26 54	.294			6,537
Suburbs	.030	1.26	22 12	.414	−55	−199	2,182
Hispanics							
Central City	.065	2.20	26.03	.393			2,882
Suburbs	.005	.09	20.53	.604	−34	−148	1,014

[a] Estimates in excess of 100 percent indicate that the central city employment rate would rise above the suburban employment rate as the result of the indicated substitution.

[b] Indicates that the central city effect is not significantly different from the suburban area effect at the 10 percent level by a two-tailed test.

displace teenagers for jobs. Higher fractions of jobs in youth-intensive occupations indicate that the metropolitan area's occupational structure is more favorable to teenagers. The relative size of the black population and the extent to which black youths encounter consumer discrimination in obtaining employment are thought to be inversely related (Becker 1971). Consumer discrimination may be particularly important in the case of youths, since many of the jobs they hold involve interaction with customers. For example, close to one-half of the number of working teenagers have jobs as sales or service workers. Finally, the population of the metropolitan area is included to capture potentially a variety of factors that vary with the size of the area and may affect youth employment. These include concern for personal safety, availability of public transportation, and variety of available jobs.

The estimated effects of a five-minute reduction in travel time on the probability of employment of central city and suburban youths are reported in table 3.9. For both white and black enrolled youths, the hypothetical improvement in job access causes the probability of having a job to roughly increase by a substantial 6 percentage points, regardless of location. For enrolled Hispanic youths, the estimated job access effect is also large within central cities, but much smaller in suburban areas.

Turning to the results obtained for nonenrolled youth, job access effects for whites are once again small—as they were for the overall sample—and virtually identical between the central city and suburban areas. For blacks and Hispanics, the central city effects are large in an absolute sense and relative to those estimated for youth living in the suburbs. Specifically, a five-minute reduction in travel time is found to increase the job probability of both groups who live within central cities by about 7 percentage points. This amounts to a 24 percent increase in the employment rate of blacks and an 18 percent increase in the employment rate of Hispanics.

The results for both enrolled and nonenrolled black youths are contrary to Wilson's first hypothesis. Job access is found to have a strong effect on the job probability of black youths living in large central cities. It may be the case, however, that Wilson's hypothesis, while not generally valid, may apply to youths living in poverty, since they are the most likely to be socially isolated from mainstream society. Additional equations were therefore estimated for those central city black youths identified by the 1980 Public-Use Sample as living in families below the poverty line. Employment rates for this group are abysmally low — .126 for enrolled youths and .158 for nonenrolled youths. The magnitudes of the job access effects estimated for poverty youths are nearly identical to those obtained for the total samples. The results obtained for the total and poverty samples of black central city youths carry considerable importance, for they suggest that the very high rate of joblessness experienced by these groups can be ameliorated by policies that improve job accessibility within central city neighborhoods.

Central city and suburban mean travel times for each youth group are considerably different. For all six race/enrollment groups, central city time is higher than suburban time, and all time differences are statistically significant at the 5 percent level. This implies that the relatively low employment rates of central city youths can be partially attributed to their inferior access to jobs. The results show that if central city youths had the same access to jobs as suburban youths, there would be large declines in the employment rate differences that exist between these two groups (see table 3.9). In fact, for black and white enrolled teenagers, the central city employment rate would actually rise above the suburban area employment rate; hence, for youths of all three racial groups, both those in and out of school, job access plays an important role in explaining lower rates of employment within central cities.

Also reported in table 3.9 are the percentage changes in the city/suburban employment rate differences that would occur if travel time had the same effect on central city youths as it has on suburban teenagers. For all but one of the minority groups, the jobs access effect is significantly larger in absolute magnitude for the central city group, as compared to the suburban group. In each case, the central city employment rate would be greater than the suburban area employment rate if travel time had the same effect on city youths as it has on suburban youths. These results suggest that the low employment rates of central city minority youths can be attributed both to their inferior job access and to job access having a stronger effect on their job probability.

Before turning to the results relating to Wilson's second hypothesis, it is of interest to consider the effects of the metropolitan area variables. The estimated change in the probability of having a job from a unit change in each of these variables is reported in table 3.10. The variable that has the most robust and strongest effect on youth employment is the area unemployment rate. It has a negative effect on the job probability of all groups. The sizes of the effects are generally larger — in absolute magnitude — for blacks and Hispanics in comparison to whites. Of particular interest is the estimated effect for nonenrolled central city black youth, since the high rate of joblessness of this group is considered to be a major social problem. A one point change in area unemployment is found to raise the employment of this group by a substantial 2.5 percentage points. Overall, my results are consistent with those obtained by Freeman (1991), who also estimated job probability equations for nonenrolled youths. He also found that tight labor markets have a strong positive effect on youth employment, and improve the employment prospects of blacks more than whites. As Freeman notes, these findings are important because they are contrary to the notion that central city black teenagers are separated from the general economy. The estimated effects of the metropolitan area unemployment rate and intraurban job accessibility on the job probability of nonenrolled black youths living within central cities tell a consistent story: the employment of these youth is strongly affected by the availability of legitimate job opportunities. The results are therefore inconsistent with, not only the notion that these youths are excluded from the general economy, but also with the idea that they are unwilling or unable to work at a low-wage job (Mead 1987).

Regarding the effects of the other area variables, an occupational structure that is more favorable to teenagers is generally found to increase their employment probability. As expected, the fraction of the labor force who are adult women has a negative effect on youth employment, but the effect is statistically significant for only the white groups. These results are interesting, since they suggest that employers view

Table 3.10   Estimated Changes in Job Probability from a Unit Change in the Metropolitan Area Variables

| | Blacks | | | | Whites | | | | Hispanics | | | |
| | Enrolled | | Not Enrolled | | Enrolled | | Not Enrolled | | Enrolled | | Enrolled | |
	Central City	Suburbs	Central City	Suburbs	Central City	Suburbs	Central City	Suburbs	Central City	Suburbs	Central City	Suburbs
COMP	−.591	−2.110	−.138	1.121	−2.198	−3.627	−2.064	−1.421	−.565	−.534	−1.700	−.096
	(1.10)	(2.60)	(.23)	(1.13)	(1.56)	(6.39)	(1.78)	(2.74)	(.78)	(.55)	(1.41)	(.06)
YJOB	.438	1.612	−.002	−.970	2.146	2.194	1.231	.924	1.546	1.481	1.276	.943
	(.99)	(2.90)	(.03)	(1.17)	(2.13)	(5.83)	(1.39)	(2.60)	(2.14)	(1.68)	(1.06)	(.62)
UNEMP	−.011	−.029	−.025	−.014	−.011	−.017	−.002	−.021	−.026	−.045	−.021	−.052
	(2.66)	(4.17)	(5.67)	(1.67)	(1.14)	(4.23)	(.24)	(6.07)	(4.04)	(3.34)	(2.06)	(2.44)
POP (10,000)	−.006	−.011	.140	.058	−.032	−.058	−.070	−.059	−.104	−.156	−.064	−.031
	(.15)	(.29)	(2.68)	(1.10)	(.35)	(1.81)	(.83)	(1.99)	(2.50)	(3.19)	(.88)	(.39)
FBLACK	.347	.535	.111	.252	−.360	.411	.238	.516	.590	−.122	.264	−.321
	(2.29)	(4.17)	(.86)	(1.11)	(1.26)	(4.37)	(.98)	(6.00)	(2.98)	(.52)	(.92)	(.83)

COMP   = fraction of the metropolitan area labor force who are women over the age of 19 who have a high school education or less.
YJOB   = fraction of the metropolitan area's jobs in youth-intensive occupations, i.e., service, laborers, operatives, sales, and clerical.
UNEMP = metropolitan area unemployment rate.
POP   = population of the metropolitan area.
FBLACK = fraction of the metropolitan area population that is black.

t-statistics are in parentheses.

less-educated adult women and white teenagers as closer substitutes for one another in making the hiring decision than they do adult women and minority teenagers.

The most noteworthy results obtained with the racial composition variable are for suburban white youths. This group is found to have a higher probability of having a job in those areas where blacks are a larger fraction of the population. This suggests that these teenagers encounter less competition for jobs from blacks than they do from other whites. The results do not suggest that blacks encounter less discrimination in metropolitan areas where their numbers are relatively larger. Finally, the population size of the metropolitan area is found to have little effect on the black groups, but has a negative effect for all white and Hispanic groups, which is statistically significant one-half of the time.

Wilson's concentration effects hypothesis implies that a residential location within a large central city will have a negative effect on a black youth's probability of having a job that is separate from the negative effect of inferior job access. This implication can be empirically investigated by first noticing that the employment rate differential between nonenrolled central city and suburban black youth can be defined as:

$$\bar{X}_c \hat{B}_c - \bar{X}_x \hat{B}_x, \tag{3.4}$$

where $\bar{X}_c$ and $\bar{X}_s$ are, respectively, the mean values of the independent variables for central city and suburban youth, and $\hat{B}_c$ and $\hat{B}_s$ are the coefficient vectors estimated from the linear probability models. This differential can be decomposed into two parts, the first representing the effects of different mean values of the independent variables and the second representing coefficient differences:

$$\bar{X}_c \hat{B}_x - \bar{X}_s \hat{B}_s = (\bar{X}_c - \bar{X}_x)\hat{B}_c + \bar{X}_x(\hat{B}_x - \hat{B}_s). \tag{3.5}$$

An estimate of the effect that a central city location has on a youth's job probability can be obtained by adding up the coefficient differences on the intercept term, the family and individual variables, and the metropolitan area variables between the central city and suburban equations.[16] The existence of concentration effects within central cities suggests that this number has a negative value.

The decomposition was done for the total sample of nonenrolled black youths and for a sample restricted to nonenrolled youths whose family incomes — net of the youth's earnings — were low (i.e., less than $20,000). The results are reported in table 3.11. The estimated central city effect for both samples is positive in magnitude, and not negative as expected. For the total sample, this effect indicates that if two identical black youths living in the same metropolitan area have the same access to jobs and are similarly affected by job access, the central city youth would have a job probability 149 percent higher than the suburban youth. The corresponding estimate obtained for the low-income sample is 176 percent.[17]

These results strongly contradict Wilson's hypothesis; however, concentration effects may, at least in part, contribute to the relatively strong job access effect observed for central city youths. For example, the willingness of these teenagers to make a long commute to a distant job

Table 3.11 Decomposition of Central City/Suburban Employment Rate Differential for Out-of-School Black Youths

	Total Sample		Low-Income Sample	
	Amount Attributable to Means	Amount Attributable to Coefficients	Amount Attributable to Means	Amount Attributable to Coefficients
Family and individual variables	−31.7	−158.3	−24.4	−61.4
Metropolitan area variables	5.7	101.7	4.5	14.6
Intercept		205.8		223.3
Subtotal	−26.0	149.2	−19.9	176.5
Travel time	−53.7	−168.3	−51.9	−204.8
Total	−79.7	−19.1	−71.8	−28.3

A + sign indicates advantage for central city youth; a − sign indicates advantage for suburban youth.

may be less if there is an absence of positive role models within the neighborhood. If the travel-time estimated coefficient difference is included in the estimation of the central city effect, the effect is now negative in sign and explains 19 percent and 28 percent of the central city/suburban area employment rate differential for the total and low-income samples, respectively. These percentages represent an upper-bound estimate of the portion of the central city/suburban area employment rate differential that may be attributable to concentration effects. Note that these percentages, while nontrivial in magnitude, are only about one-half as large as the portions of the employment rate differences that result from differential access to jobs.

Summary and Conclusions

This chapter has presented the findings obtained from a thorough investigation of the effect of intraurban job accessibility on youth employment. Separate estimates of the effect of job access on job probability were provided for many different groups of youths in order to answer six specific questions. The first asked whether our Philadelphia results overstated the importance of job access as one explanation for racial differences in youth employment rates. The evidence presented suggests these results are representative of the role that job access plays in very large cities. The results, however, also suggest that job access is somewhat less important in explaining differences in black and white employment rates at the national level.

The second question addressed whether differential job accessibility is capable of explaining any of the difference that exists between the employment rates of white and Hispanic youths. The evidence presented suggests that job access does indeed play an important role in explaining the relatively low employment rates of Hispanic youths. The explanatory power of job access is about the same for Hispanics as for blacks.

The third question I attempted to answer concerned the relationship between the strength of the job access effect and family income. Theory does not yield a clear prediction regarding the sign of this relationship.

The evidence presented suggests that the magnitude of the effect of job access on youth employment does not vary with family income for most groups. In addition, since the difference in expected travel times of youth from low- and high-income families is small relative to interracial differences, job access plays a relatively modest role for minority youths, and virtually no role for white youths in explaining the tendency for teenage employment rates to rise with the level of family income.

The fourth question investigated whether the importance of job access as an explanation for racial differences in youth employment rates differs between large and small metropolitan areas. The results indicate that the answer to this question is a definite yes, with job access playing a much more significant role in larger SMSAs.

The fifth question asked whether the higher employment rates observed for youths living in smaller SMSAs can be attributed, at least in part, to this group possessing superior access to jobs. The evidence indicated that large portions of the employment rate differentials that exist between small and large SMSAs can be attributed to differences in job access.

The final question involved estimating separate equations for youths living in central city and suburban areas. The poorer job access of central city youths was found to play a substantial role in explaining their lower employment rates. Of particular interest were the findings for central city and suburban black teenagers who are not in school: (1) the effect of job access on job probability is stronger for central city in comparison to suburban youth; and (2) after controlling for area differences in job accessibility, residing in a central city results in a higher probability of having a job. The conclusion implied by these results is that it is poor job access, and not the existence of concentration effects, that is fundamental to our understanding of why joblessness among black youths is higher in central cities, as compared to suburban areas.

NOTES

[1] Our analysis of the black youth employment problem based on Philadelphia data is reviewed in chapter 2.

[2] Taeuber's index of residential segregation was 88 for the city of Philadelphia in 1980 (Taeuber 1983). A value of 100 indicates complete segregation of the races. In comparison, the national average value of the segregation index for 28 central cities in 1980 was 81.

[3] Wilson suggests that it is the central city black youth's lack of access to the job network that explains why Ellwood's results for Chicago failed to support the spatial mismatch hypothesis (see chapter 2 for a review of Ellwood's study).

[4] A second measure of job access was also used. This measure was constructed in the same manner as T_i, except that low-wage workers were replaced by workers in youth-intensive occupational groups. More detail on the construction of this variable is provided in chapter 4. The results obtained with this alternative travel-time variable are very similar to those obtained with T_i; hence, in the interest of keeping the present chapter of manageable length, these additional results are not presented. However, the multinomial logit results obtained with both measures of job access are reported in chapter 4.

[5] The average number of workers used to compute the mean zonal travel time was 500, 80, and 40 in the case of whites, blacks, and Hispanics, respectively. The relatively low number counts available for Hispanics suggest that for them T_i is measured with greater error.

[6] I found that the jobs-to-workers ratios had a positive and statistically significant effect on job probability; however, the magnitude of these effects and their contribution to explanatory power were smaller than those obtained with travel time.

[7] If travel times were not standardized for mode of transportation, differences in mean travel time among zones would reflect both the distances to jobs and mode choices, since travel time per unit distance is higher for public in comparison to private transportation. On the other hand, mean travel time by private carrier may be a poor proxy for job access if mode choice strongly depends upon the distance travelled. In McFadden's (1974) comprehensive analysis of urban travel demand, distance to work and choice of mode were found to be only weakly correlated. Private rather than public transportation times were used as the measure of job access, because most zones contained too few public transit riders to compute a reliable average.

[8] There are three possible problems with using mean travel time of the residential zone as the measure of job access. First, there may be a weak correlation between the number of workers who commute to nearby jobs and the number of nearby job vacancies. This will be true if workers have a strong attachment to their present jobs so that there is little turnover. However, since the low-wage jobs held by the workers in the samples used to compute times are characterized by high turnover, mean travel time should reliably measure the expected commute of the marginal worker.

A second concern is that mean travel time may serve as a proxy for influences other than job access. For example, suburban employers may be less willing to hire blacks who reside within ghettos, because residential location is used as an indicator of the worker's expected productivity or reliability. Since mean travel time is generally higher for ghetto blacks, there may be a negative correlation between travel time and job probability that is independent of the effect of job access. This would lead to biased estimates of the job access effect. There are two pieces of evidence that suggest that this bias is not an important concern. First, as reported in chapter 4, equations were run that included additional independent variables that measured the socioeconomic characteristics of the population living within the residential zone. They included the mean educational level of the male population over the age of 25, the percentage of the population that is black, and the percentage of the population below the poverty line. These variables were generally not significant and their inclusion had little effect on the results obtained with travel time. Second, if travel time affected job probability because employers use residential location as a screening device, we would expect that estimated travel time coefficients would be consistently lower for whites than blacks. The results reported in this chapter and in chapter 4 are contrary to this expectation. In most cases, the effect of travel time on the probability of a youth having a job is similar between whites and blacks.

A final concern with the use of the mean travel time of the residential zone as the measure of job access has been noted by Moulton (1990). He has shown that standard errors on aggregate variables in microdata models may be understated if the disturbance is correlated within the groups used to define the aggregate variables. Intuitively, the idea is that within-group correlation implies that an additional micro observation within the same group does not yield as much new information as would be obtained from truly independent observations. To test for this problem, Moulton and Randolph (1989) suggest using an F-test for the significance of adding a set of group dummies to the microdata regression. To conduct this test, I estimated equations that included a set of dummy variables for the 400 residential zones used to measure travel time. None of the F values were statistically significant at conventional levels. In addition, models were estimated that allowed for the variance components structure of the disturbance. These results were very similar to those presented in the text. Finally, corrected OLS standard errors were estimated for the linear probability models. These standard errors were never more than 15 percent larger than the uncorrected standard errors, and making these corrections had virtually no effect on inferences drawn from tests of significance. I owe a special debt of gratitude to Moulton for helping me estimate the variance components models and the corrected standard errors.

[9] As an alternative to controlling for these factors, independent variables describing the labor markets of each metropolitan area could have been included. In fact, this is the approach taken later in this chapter, when samples are divided into central city and suburban observations. However, since the primary focus of the analysis is on the effect of intraurban job accessibility on youth employment, the use of metropolitan area dummy variables is the preferred approach, since they capture influences that may be missed by the inclusion of labor market descriptors.

[10] Among the SMSAs selected are 40 of the largest 50 metropolitan areas in population size. The 50 SMSAs represented in the samples account for 56 percent of the total 1980 U.S. metropolitan area population.

[11] The residential zones are labelled 'county groups' in the 1980 Public-Use Sample technical documentation and consist of central cities and suburban areas that contain a minimum population of 100,000. For smaller SMSAs, county groups in the suburbs are comprised of more than one county. For larger SMSAs, less-populated counties are separate county groups, while larger counties are divided into two or more county groups.

[12] The OLS and logit results were similar in the sense that the estimated OLS coefficients on travel time and the partial derivatives of job probability with respect to travel time implied by the estimated logit coefficients were virtually identical. The implied partial derivatives were computed at the mean values of the independent variables.

[13] For selected groups, separate equations were also estimated for males and females. The results were judged sufficiently similar between the sexes that separate analyses were not required.

[14] The black-white difference in the mean value of travel time is 3.5 (4.5) minutes greater in New York (Chicago) than it is in Philadelphia.

[15] OLS was used to generate these results. The interaction variables estimate the difference in the effect of travel time between the lowest income group (the reference category) and the higher income groups.

[16] For a proof of equation (3.5) see Oaxaca (1973) or Blinder (1973). Typically, it is the employment-rate (or wage-rate) differential between blacks and whites or between males and females that is decomposed using Blinder's or Oaxaca's technique. My estimate of the central city effect is analogous to the race or gender effect estimated in these studies. Frequently, the finding of a nontrivial race or gender effect is attributed to discrimination in the labor market.

[17] There are a number of possible explanations for finding that the central city residual effect is positive. First, there is the "sheltered workplace hypothesis," discussed in chapter 2. According to this hypothesis, blacks encounter less consumer discrimination in the central city, because consumers are more likely to be black. Second, black youths living in the central city may face less competition for jobs from white youths. This will result in higher black employment in the central city than in the suburbs if employers prefer to hire whites over blacks. Such a preference could be based on prejudice or the perception that whites are more qualified to work than blacks. Third, there is the "theory of relative deprivation," which is the antithesis of Wilson's "concentration effects hypothesis." According to this theory, black youth will have greater self-confidence and competitive drive if they reside in neighborhoods where their abilities are in line with those of the representative youth. If they live in neighborhoods where they are surrounded by youth of higher socioeconomic status, they may feel inferior and drop out of the competition for jobs. Unfortunately, little evidence of a reliable nature exists on the above three hypotheses; however, see Ihlanfeldt and Sjoquist (1991b) for evidence in support of the sheltered workplace hypothesis.

APPENDIX TO CHAPTER 3

Areas Included in Samples and Results for Teenagers

Table 3A.1   Metropolitan Areas Included in the Youth Samples

Metropolitan Area	Number of Residential Zones	Sample (A or B)[1]
Albany, New York	5	A
Allentown, Pennsylvania	4	A
Anaheim, California	12	B
Atlanta, Georgia	6	A
Baltimore, Maryland	5	A
Boston, Massachusetts	14	A
Chicago, Illinois	32	B
Cincinnati, Ohio	5	A
Cleveland, Ohio	10	A
Dallas, Texas	13	A
Dayton, Ohio	5	A
Denver, Colorado	7	A
Detroit, Michigan	25	A
Ft. Lauderdale, Florida	7	A
Gary, Indiana	4	A
Grand Rapids, Michigan	4	A
Greensboro, North Carolina	5	A
Harrisburg, Pennsylvania	4	A
Hartford, Connecticut	5	B
Houston, Texas	6	A
Indianapolis, Indiana	4	A
Kansas City, Missouri	7	A
Long Branch, California	4	A
Los Angeles, California	28	B
Miami, Florida	10	A
Milwaukee, Wisconsin	4	A
Minneapolis, Minnesota	11	A
Nashville, Tennessee	4	A
Nassau, New York	19	B
Newark, New Jersey	15	A
New Brunswick, New Jersey	4	A
New Orleans, Louisiana	6	A
New York, New York	13	A
Norfolk, Virginia	4	A
Northeast Pennsylvania	5	A
Oklahoma City, Oklahoma	4	A

Table 3A.1 (*continued*)

Metropolitan Area	Number of Residential Zones	Sample (A or B)[1]
Philadelphia, Pennsylvania	26	A
Pittsburgh, Pennsylvania	11	A
Portland, Oregon	4	A
Providence, Rhode Island	5	B
Riverside, California	6	B
Sacramento, California	4	A
Saint Louis, Missouri	8	A
Salt Lake, Utah	4	A
San Diego, California	5	B
San Francisco, California	6	A
San Jose, California	5	B
Tampa, Florida	6	A
Washington, D.C.	7	A
Youngstown, Ohio	4	A

[1] Sample A is the 5 percent sample of the 1980 Public-Use Microdata Sample.
Sample B is the 1 percent sample of the 1980 Public-Use Microdata Sample.

Table 3A.2   Means (Standard Deviations) of Individual and Family Variables for Teenager (16–19 Years Old) Samples

	Whites		Blacks		Hispanics	
	Enrolled	**Not Enrolled**	**Enrolled**	**Not Enrolled**	**Enrolled**	**Not Enrolled**
Age of youth	17.065	18.230	17.080	18.163	17.089	18.010
	(1.002)	(.864)	(1.019)	(.912)	(1.026)	(.998)
Years of school	12.466	13.142	12.212	12.558	12.151	11.781
	(1.211)	(1.633)	(1.346)	(2.042)	(1.468)	(2.663)
Spouse present	.003	.036	.008	.021	.011	.063
	(.058)	(.185)	(.089)	(.143)	(.103)	(.243)
Good health	.978	.965	.975	.955	.977	.963
	(.144)	(.184)	(.154)	(.207)	(.147)	(.187)
Female	.478	.468	.509	.491	.503	.441
	(.499)	(.499)	(.499)	(.499)	(.500)	(.497)
High school diploma	.166	.641	.138	.437	.153	.344
	(.372)	(.480)	(.345)	(.496)	(.360)	(.475)
Borne a child	.004	.030	.049	.171	.013	.076
	(.064)	(.172)	(.215)	(.376)	(.114)	(.265)
Female head	.134	.191	.461	.535	.258	.281
	(.341)	(.393)	(.498)	(.499)	(.438)	(.450)
Head's years of school	15.130	13.587	12.911	12.184	11.783	10.103
	(3.193)	(3.012)	(3.254)	(3.111)	(4.590)	(4.557)
Family income net of youth's earnings (reference category=less than $10,000)						
$10,000 to $20,000	.162	.236	.299	.299	.279	.292
	(.369)	(.424)	(.458)	(.457)	(.448)	(.455)
$20,000 to $30,000	.259	.279	.196	.175	.235	.212
	(.439)	(.449)	(.397)	(.380)	(.424)	(.409)
$30,000 to $40,000	.229	.196	.105	.077	.128	.106
	(.421)	(.397)	(.307)	(.267)	(.334)	(.308)
$40,000+	.272	.170	.079	.050	.100	.062
	(.445)	(.376)	(.269)	(.217)	(.300)	(.242)
Occupation of household head (reference category=head without a job)						
Manager or professional	.328	.181	.102	.064	.139	.078
	(.469)	(.385)	(.303)	(.244)	(.346)	(.268)
Technical, sales, or administrative support	.217	.195	.151	.130	.136	.104
	(.412)	(.396)	(.358)	(.336)	(.343)	(.305)
Service	.056	.081	.152	.163	.107	.119
	(.230)	(.273)	(.359)	(.370)	(.309)	(.324)
Craftsman	.179	.218	.093	.082	.163	.162
	(.383)	(.413)	(.290)	(.275)	(.370)	(.368)
Laborer	.121	.176	.193	.195	.219	.250
	(.326)	(.381)	(.395)	(.396)	.413)	(.433)

**Table 3A.3   Linear Probability Model Results for Teenagers
(Absolute Value of *t*-statistic in Parentheses)**

	Whites		Blacks		Hispanics	
	Enrolled	**Not Enrolled**	**Enrolled**	**Not Enrolled**	**Enrolled**	**Not Enrolled**
Travel time	−.012	−.005	−.010	−.012	−.009	−.006
	(4.298)	(1.137)	(5.730)	(3.414)	(4.300)	(1.523)
Age of youth	.062	.067	.045	.070	.051	.087
	(7.734)	(5.948)	(8,686)	(7.653)	(7.727)	(9.926)
Years of school	.078	.010	.045	.070	.051	.087
	(11.202)	(1.149)	(6.022)	(1.195)	(7.079)	(2.878)
Spouse present	−.079	−.087	.014	.027	−.015	−.030
	(.890)	(1.773)	(.311)	(.502)	(.295)	(8.42)
Good health	.114	.208	.030	.124	.113	.199
	(3.196)	(.4333)	(1.181)	(3.266)	(3.259)	(4.512)
Female	−.001	−.017	−.009	−.031	−.028	−.052
	(.112)	(.979)	(1.148)	(1.723)	(2.779)	(2.979)
High school diploma	−.109	.205	.011	.152	.035	.118
	(5.478)	(7.116)	(.728)	(6.969)	(1.814)	(5.060)
Borne a child	−.137	−.331	−.064	−.136	−.098	−.225
	(1.700)	(6.229)	(3.433)	(5.730)	(2.157)	(6.564)
Female head	.018	.007	−.003	−.013	−.098	−.225
	(1.043)	(.291)	(.281)	(.707)	(1.580)	(.339)
Head's years of school	−.008	−.004	−.000	−.005	.001	.001
	(3.711)	(1.315)	(.491)	(1.760)	(.912)	(.220)

*Family income net of youth's earnings
(reference category=less than $10,000)*

	Whites		Blacks		Hispanics	
	Enrolled	**Not Enrolled**	**Enrolled**	**Not Enrolled**	**Enrolled**	**Not Enrolled**
$10,000 to $20,000	.089	−.004	.013	.034	.014	.035
	(3.814)	(.135)	(1.176)	(1.715)	(.893)	(1.564)
$20,000 to $30,000	.091	−.004	.013	.034	.014	.035
	(3.899)	(1.621)	(2.489)	(1.740)	(1.291)	(1.986)
$30,000 to $40,000	.107	.085	.045	.054	.064	.119
	(4.404)	(2.403)	(2.829)	(1.601)	(3.148)	(3.708)
$40,000+	.065	.075	.036	.070	.029	.163
	(2.613)	(2.003)	(2.007)	(1.736)	(1.282)	(4.177)

Table 3A.3 (*continued*)

	Whites		Blacks		Hispanics	
	Enrolled	**Not Enrolled**	**Enrolled**	**Not Enrolled**	**Enrolled**	**Not Enrolled**
Occupation of household head (reference category=head without a job)						
Manager or professional	.076 (3.494)	.053 (1.588)	.044 (2.705)	.093 (2.595)	.019 (.944)	.104 (2.846)
Technical, sales, or administrative support	.095 (4.451)	.039 (1.253)	.037 (2.778)	.132 (4.954)	.056 (2.932)	.053 (1.668)
Service	.022 (.804)	.077 (2.049)	.039 (3.126)	.079 (3.330)	.066 (3.358)	.079 (2.736)
Craftsmen	.070 (3.237)	.043 (1.419)	.014 (.874)	.103 (3.202)	.028 (1.531)	.082 (2.903)
Laborer	.060 (2.593)	.040 (1.268)	.000 (.003)	.055 (2.307)	.051 (3.055)	.085 (3.489)
Intercept	−1.540 (11.071)	−.885 (3.650)	−.794 (8.281)	−.933 (4.718)	−1.049 (8.374)	−1.249 (6.340)
R-square	.095	.179	.076	.150	.114	.174
Obs.	8,500	2,492	9,400	3,296	7,314	3,234

Table 3A.4 Dichotomous Logit Model Results for Teenagers (Absolute Value of *t*-statistic in Parentheses)

	Whites		Blacks		Hispanics	
	Enrolled	**Not Enrolled**	**Enrolled**	**Not Enrolled**	**Enrolled**	**Not Enrolled**
Travel time	−.059	−.029	−.006	−.059	−.052	−.028
	(4.543)	(1.075)	(6.041)	(3.480)	(4.710)	(1.530)
Age of youth	.215	.349	.290	.413	.247	.416
	(5.657)	(5.816)	(7.837)	(7.942)	(6.712)	(9.674)
Years of school	.450	.044	.243	.048	.246	.055
	(11.538)	(.977)	(6.621)	(1.500)	(7.454)	(2.806)
Spouse present	−.360	−.446	.098	.198	−.050	−.119
	(.880)	(1.708)	(.316)	(.702)	(.184)	(.688)
Good health	.584	1.034	.269	.780	.818	1.053
	(3.262)	(4.055)	(1.358)	(3.291)	(3.437)	(4.393)
Female	−.014	−.099	−.065	−.163	−.152	−.252
	(.298)	(.990)	(1.140)	(1.772)	(2.763)	(3.000)
High school diploma	−.598	1.020	−.148	.700	−.007	.542
	(6.535)	(6.710)	(1.451)	(5.932)	(.070)	(4.927)
Borne a child	−.637	−1.700	−.506	−.850	−.670	1.213
	(1.641)	(5.492)	(3.373)	(6.204)	(2.233)	(6.459)
Female head	.088	.043	−.020	.079	.111	.028
	(1.086)	(.309)	(.289)	(.814)	(1.405)	(.269)
Head's years of school	−.035	−.023	−.005	−.027	.006	.003
	(3.888)	(1.240)	(.555)	(1.901)	(.857)	(.309)
Family income net of youth's earnings (reference category=less than $10,000)						
$10,000 to $20,000	.439	−.030	.109	.183	.099	.170
	(3.990)	(.180)	(1.410)	(1.743)	(1.138)	(1.604)
$20,000 to $30,000	.451	.285	.242	.216	.140	.235
	(4.063)	(1.601)	(2.630)	(1.700)	(1.478)	(1.926)
$30,000 to $40,000	.523	.469	.315	.253	.337	.563
	(4.548)	(2.417)	(2.866)	(1.479)	(3.091)	(3.680)
$40,000+	.332	.417	.264	.331	.162	.766
	(2.862)	(2.014)	(2.146)	(1.647)	(1.361)	(4.010)

Table 3A.4   (*continued*)

	Whites		Blacks		Hispanics	
	Enrolled	**Not Enrolled**	**Enrolled**	**Not Enrolled**	**Enrolled**	**Not Enrolled**
Occupation of household head (reference category=head without a job)						
Manager or professional	.359 (3.592)	.288 (1.548)	.289 (2.580)	.510 (2.833)	.147 (1.300)	.482 (2.754)
Technical sales, or administrative support	.477 (4.597)	.205 (1.220)	.267 (2.840)	.716 (2.833)	.329 (1.300)	.269 (2.754)
Service	.127 (.992)	.433 (2.072)	.290 (3.258)	.465 (3.750)	.421 (3.841)	.395 (2.862)
Craftsmen	.342 (3.386)	.222 (1.329)	.119 (1.062)	.557 (3.460)	.197 (1.913)	.401 (2.993)
Laborer	.299 (2.804)	.207 (1.210)	.011 (.121)	.330 (2.640)	.320 (3.404)	.414 (3.600)
Intercept	−9.304 (14.419)	−7.064 (5.308)	−8.827 (12.792)	−8.626 (7.702)	−8.593 (12.140)	−8.495 (8.677)
Chi-square	10,531	2,629	8,124	3,616	7,820	3,831
Obs.	8,500	2,492	9,400	3,296	7,314	3,234

4

The Impact of Intraurban Job Accessibility on the School Enrollment and Employment Decisions of Teenagers
A Multinomial Logit Analysis

In the previous chapter the effect of intraurban job accessibility on youth employment was investigated by estimating job-probability equations that treated the school enrollment decision as exogenous.[1] In this chapter, the results obtained from estimating less restrictive models that allow for the joint endogeneity of the work and enrollment decisions are presented. The motivation underlying the analysis included in this chapter is twofold. First, it is of interest to determine whether the strong job access effects on youth employment reported in the previous chapter hold up when the enrollment decision is treated as endogenous. This continues the inquiry of chapter 3 regarding the robustness of my results. Second, from a policy perspective, it is crucial to determine whether job access affects a youth's decision to drop out of school. On the one hand, since an improvement in job access increases a teenager's opportunity cost of staying in high school, there may exist an undesirable tradeoff between employment and enrollment. On the other hand, better job access may enable youths desirous of income to work part time while enrolled in school. Without part-time job opportunities located nearby, these youths may drop out, either to search for full-time employment or to engage in illicit income-producing activity. The issue of how job access affects school enrollment can therefore only be settled by empirical investigation.

The results presented in this chapter show that job accessibility has a strong effect on the probability of employment of each race-sex group and that better job access does not encourage youths to drop out of high

105

school. For younger teenagers (aged 16 to 17), job access is found to have a neutral effect on the school enrollment decision. For most of the groups of older teenagers (aged 18 to 19), an improvement in job access is observed to increase the probability of the enrolled-employed state and reduce the probability of the not enrolled-not employed state. Hence, there is an increase in school enrollment and a decrease in the likelihood that a youth is in the state that is probably most inimical to his/her own welfare and that of society.

The remainder of this chapter is organized as follows. In the next section, a theoretical model is presented that yields a multinomial logit estimating equation. The third section describes the empirical methodology. The fourth section analyzes the results obtained with the intraurban measures of job accessibility. In addition to the measures of job access, the multinomial logit equations contain an extensive set of control variables that describe the individual, his/her family background, and the metropolitan area labor market. The estimated effects of these variables on the teenager's employment and enrollment decisions are discussed in the fifth section. The final section of the chapter provides a summary and the conclusions.

Theoretical Framework

The enrollment/employment outcomes of teenagers are defined to include four mutually exclusive states: enrolled-employed, enrolled-not employed, not enrolled-employed, and not enrolled-not employed. The individual is assumed to select the state that maximizes his/her lifetime utility. The teenager's life is divided into two discrete time periods. The initial period (a) is the years that the teenager is in high school or, in the case of a dropout, the years that he/she would have been in high school had he/she continued his/her education. The second period (b) is the rest of the individual's life. The objective of the teenager is therefore to maximize

$$U_{ij} = \alpha_j E_{ij}^a + \beta_j [E_{ij}^b/(l+r)] + \epsilon_{ij}, \qquad (4.1)$$

where U_{ij} is the lifetime utility of the $_j th$ teenager associated with the $_i th$ employment-enrollment outcome, α_j and β_j are the average values attached to the present value (r is the market rate of discount) of expected earnings (E) before and after the high school years, and ϵ_{ij} is an individual-specific term. The terms α_j and β_j are, in other words, parameters of a representative teenager's utility function. Expected earnings in each time period is equal to the probability of finding employment times the expected wage rate. E^b is assumed to be higher for those individuals who finish high school (i.e., for those who select the enrolled-employed or enrolled-not employed options).

Holding other factors constant, a variable that increases the utility of one of the states will alter the enrollment-employment outcomes of teenagers at the margin and thereby increase the number of teenagers observed in that state. One variable that can be theoretically linked to the utilities of the alternative states is the nearness of available and qualifiable jobs to the teenager's residence. If jobs are located nearby, the utilities of the two employment states (i.e., enrolled-employed and not enrolled-employed) are higher because both the expected probability of finding a job and the expected wage rate are higher.

The former is higher because, as Holzer (1987) has documented, youths rely primarily on informal methods of job search, namely, checking with friends and relatives, and applying directly without referrals, which suggests that information about available job opportunities may decay rapidly with distance from home. The expected wage is higher, since the relevant wage is net of commuting costs and better job proximity implies a shorter required commute. In comparison to workers earning higher wages, this effect may be particularly strong for the typical teenager, since for any given distance, travel costs are a higher percentage of earnings, and his/her travel time is greater because he/she more frequently must rely on slower modes of transportation, for example, walking, bicycling, or taking a bus.

Equation (4.1) suggests that the effect of better job access on the four enrollment- employment states will depend on the value attached to first period (α_j) relative to second period earnings (β_j). Teenagers who place a low value on first-period earnings are more likely to be on the margin between the enrolled-employed and enrolled-not employed states. Better job access is therefore expected to cause an increase in the probability of being in the enrolled-employed state and to cause a corresponding decrease in the probability of being in the enrolled-not employed state. Teenagers who place a high value on first-period earnings are more likely to be on the margin between the enrolled-employed state and the not enrolled-employed state.

Since an improvement in job access increases the utility of both of these states, the effect on school enrollment will depend on the relative magnitudes of these increases. On the one hand, the increase in the expected wage from better job access is expected to be larger for youths in school, because their greater time commitments suggest that (1) the opportunity cost of their travel time is greater, and (2) they are able to amortize their travel costs over fewer work hours per day. This suggests that the utility associated with the enrolled-employed state will increase the most. On the other hand, the increase in expected earnings from better job access increases the opportunity cost of staying in school, which suggests that the utility associated with the not enrolled-employed state will increase the most. The effect of better job access on teenagers who are on the margin between the enrolled-employed and not enrolled-employed states is, therefore, *a priori* ambiguous.

Teenagers who place a high value on first-period earnings are also more likely to be on the margins between the two employment states and the not enrolled-not employed state. The not enrolled-not employed state includes teenagers who are engaging in illicit income-producing activity, youths searching for work, and youths who are idle. Since better job access increases the utility of the two employment states relative to the not enrolled-not employed state, the expectation is that the probability of being in the latter state will decline. School enrollment may or may not increase, depending upon how the corresponding increase in probability is divided between the enrolled and not-enrolled employment states.

In summary, the above theory predicts that teenagers who place a relatively low value on first-period earnings will experience an increase in the probability of being in the enrolled-employed state and a decrease in the probability of being in the enrolled-not employed state in response to an improvement in job access. The probability of being in school is, therefore, not expected to be affected. For teenagers who place a relatively high value on first-period earnings, the analysis suggests that the probability of being in the not enrolled-not employed state will decrease. Since the increase in probability may be for either the enrolled-employed state or the not enrolled-employed state, the probability of being in school may be affected, but the direction of the change cannot be predicted.

Since the analysis suggests that the effect of better job access on the enrollment-employment outcomes of teenagers will depend on the value attached to first-period in comparison to second-period earnings (α_j/β_j), in order to determine how the sample should be stratified for the purposes of estimation, this ratio needs to be related to identifiable characteristics of individual teenagers. I, therefore, hypothesize that the ratio is higher for youths with lower family income, higher for older teenagers, and higher for male teenagers. The relative value of α_j is hypothesized to be larger for teenagers with less family income (net of any earnings of the teenager) because, as suggested by Ehrenberg and Marcus (1982), these youths may be required to make a minimum contribution to the family budget. In addition, they may receive less transfer income from other family members and therefore have a higher marginal utility of earned income.

The expectations that the relative value of α_j is larger for older and male teenagers are based on observed labor force participation rates of teenagers who do not have high school diplomas. As indicated in table 4.1, older teenagers (18 to 19 years old) have rates of participation roughly 20 percentage points higher than younger teenagers (16 to 17 years old) within each race/sex group. Participation rates differ less by gender than by age, but for each race/age group males have higher rates than females. The higher labor force participation rates of older and male teenagers suggest that they have a greater preference for work in

Table 4.1 Labor Force Participation Rates of Teenagers Without High School Diplomas (percent)

	16–17 Years Old	18–19 Years Old
Whites		
Males	44.0	66.5
Females	40.6	57.0
Blacks		
Males	23.3	44.8
Females	20.1	33.1

SOURCE: U.S. Bureau of Census (1983a, 1983b).

the first time period (i.e., a higher relative value of $\alpha_j)^2$ A second piece of evidence also suggests that the ratio, (α_j/β_j) is higher for male in comparison to female teenagers; namely, when high school dropouts are surveyed, males consistently give economically related reasons for leaving school two to three times more often than females (Ekstrom et al. 1986; Morgan 1984; Rumberger 1983).[3]

To obtain an estimating equation, the utility of individual j in the *ith* enrollment-employment state can be expressed as:

$$U_{ij}=\gamma_i'X_j+\epsilon_{ij}, \tag{4.2}$$

where X includes a measure of intraurban job accessibility and appropriate controls and ϵ_{ij} reflects intrinsically random choice behavior and measurement error. The unobservable utility level of person j is given by:

$$U_j=\max\{U_{1j}, U_{2j}, U_{3j}, U_{4j}\}. \tag{4.3}$$

The indicator function of the observable outcome for person j can therefore be defined as:

$$I_{ij}=\begin{cases}1 \text{ if } U_j=U_{ij} & i=1,2,3,4\ldots \\ 0 \text{ otherwise}\end{cases} \tag{4.4}$$

If the ϵ_{ij} are independently and identically distributed with Wiebull density functions, then the choice probability for enrollment-employment outcome 1 is

$$P_{1j} = Prob(I_{ij}=1) = \frac{e^{\gamma_1' X_j}}{\sum_{i=1}^{4} e^{\gamma_i' X_j}} \cdot \qquad (4.5)$$

Equation (4.5) is a multinomial logit model.

Empirical Methodology

The data source used to conduct the multinomial logit analysis is once again the 1980 Public-Use Sample. Random samples of teenagers were taken from the same 50 SMSAs that formed samples 1 and 2 of chapter 3 (see table 3A.1).[4] Recall that these are the metropolitan areas for which the 1980 Public-Use Sample identifies a minimum of four intraurban residential zones. The samples consist of 16 to 19-year-olds who have not graduated from high school and who live with one or both parents or a guardian. Equations were estimated for 12 separate samples — three racial groups by two gender groups by two age groups, 16 to 17-year-olds and 18 to 19-year-olds.[5] For all groups, except 18 to 19-year-old male and female Hispanics, the sample size equaled 5,000 observations. The sample sizes for older Hispanic teenagers included roughly 2,000 observations, which equalled the total number of Hispanic teenagers available on the 1980 Public-Use Sample tapes that met the selection criteria.

The measures of job access were the same as those used in estimating the job-probability equations of chapter 3. Recall that the first measure is the one-way commuting time to work by low-wage workers who travelled to work by private, motorized carrier, and who lived in the same residential zone and were of the same race as the individual youth. The second measure of job access is constructed in the same manner as the first, except that low-wage workers are replaced by workers in youth-intensive occupational groups. An occupation is defined as youth-intensive if the percentage of the workers in the occupation who are teenagers is greater than the percentage of the total workforce who are teenagers. Since occupational segregation between the sexes exists even for teenagers, travel times were computed separately for males and females.

For female teenagers, the youth-intensive occupational groups consist of clerical workers, sales workers, and service workers. For male teenagers, they are laborers, sales workers, and service workers. The mean values of the two travel-time measures of job access broken down by race, age, sex, and family income are given in table 4.2. These values reveal that travel time (i.e., job access) differs little by age or sex. Travel time also does not vary much with the level of family income, except in the case of Hispanics, where youths with less than $10,000 in family income have higher travel times than youths with incomes greater than this amount. Concerning racial differences in travel time, for all possible comparisons, black times are five to seven minutes higher—or in percentage terms, about 35 percent greater—than the corresponding white times. Differences between Hispanic and white times decline as the level of family income rises, but in all cases the Hispanic times are larger. The travel times reported in table 4.2 are consistent with those presented in the previous chapter, in that both sets of numbers indicate that minority youth have decidedly worse access to jobs than whites.

The control variables consisted of the same personal and family background variables that entered the job-probability equations of chapter 3[6] and a set of metropolitan area descriptors that are similar to those used to estimate the effect of job access on youths living in central city and suburban areas in the sixth section of chapter 3.[7] (For the reader's convenience, all of the independent variables included in the logit runs are defined in table 4.3.)[8]

As indicated above, separate equations were estimated for 12 groups defined on the basis of age, gender, and race. However, the theoretical analysis suggested that the effect of job access on the enrollment-employment outcomes of teenagers may also vary with the level of family income. Since additional stratification of the sample would have resulted in a considerable increase in computational cost—and small sample sizes for some groups, especially Hispanics—the travel time variables were constructed to allow the job access effect to vary with family income within each equation. This was accomplished by first

**Table 4.2 Mean Value of the Expected Travel Time
by Auto Assigned to Each Teenager**

| | Males | | | | Females | | | |
| | 16–17 Years Old | | 18–19 Years Old | | 16–17 Years Old | | 18–19 Years Old | |
	$T1$[a]	$T2$	$T1$	$T2$	$T1$	$T2$	$T1$	$T2$
Whites								
$Y1$[b]	18.8	17.9	18.8	17.9	18.8	19.3	18.8	19.3
$Y2$	18.8	17.9	18.7	17.5	18.7	19.2	18.6	19.1
$Y3$	18.5	17.6	18.6	17.5	18.6	19.2	18.6	19.1
$Y4$	18.6	17.6	18.6	17.5	18.6	19.3	18.5	19.2
Blacks								
$Y1$	24.5	24.4	24.6	24.5	24.4	24.2	24.6	24.3
$Y2$	24.0	23.7	24.2	24.0	24.1	24.0	24.4	24.2
$Y3$	23.9	23.6	23.9	23.6	23.8	23.8	24.1	24.0
$Y4$	23.4	22.9	23.9	23.7	23.8	23.9	23.5	23.6
Hispanics								
$Y1$	24.6	24.0	24.4	23.7	24.6	24.3	25.1	24.8
$Y2$	22.2	21.5	22.6	21.8	22.6	22.3	22.7	22.3
$Y3$	21.5	20.8	21.7	21.1	21.4	21.2	22.1	21.7
$Y4$	21.0	20.1	21.5	20.7	20.9	20.8	21.1	20.8

[a] $T1$ = travel time of low-wage workers, $T2$ = travel time of workers in youth-intensive occupations.

[b] $Y1, \ldots Y4$ represent annual family income for the year 1979 net of the youth's earnings. $0 \leq Y1 \leq \$15,000$; $\$15,000 < Y2 \leq \$25,000$; $\$25,000 < Y3 \leq \$35,000$; $Y4 > \$35,000$.

defining four income categories: $0 \leq Y1 \leq \$15,000$; $\$15,000 < Y2 \leq \$25,000$; $\$25,000 < Y3 \leq \$35,000$; and $Y4 > \$35,000$, where $Y1, \ldots Y4$ represent annual family income for the year 1979 net of the youth's earnings. If income was in the first category, then the time variable equalled the mean value of the residential zone and otherwise it equalled zero. The same procedure was followed for the other three income groups.

Before presenting the results obtained from estimating the multinomial logit models, it is instructive to consider the distribution of teenagers among the four enrollment-employment states. These per-

**Table 4.3 Definitions of Independent Variables
Used in the Multinomial Logit Analysis**

Job Accessibility Measures

   (1) Mean one-way travel time of low-wage workers (wage rate $\leq \$5.00$) who travel to work by private, motorized carrier and who live in the same residential zone as teenager.

   (2) Same as (1), except low-wage workers are replaced by workers in youth-intensive occupations. For males, youth-intensive occupations include laborers, service workers, and sales workers. For females, these occupations are clerical workers, service workers, and sales workers.

Personal Characteristics

   (1) Age of youth in years.

   (2) Years of school completed.

   (3) Spouse of youth present in household (yes $=1$).

   (4) Youth has no mental or physical problems limiting the type of work (yes $=1$).

   (5) Youth has borne a child (yes $=1$).

Family Background

   (1) Residence in one-parent−female-headed family (yes $=1$).

   (2) Completed years of education of head of household.

   (3) Annual family income of 1979 minus the youth's earnings.

   (4) Annual family income squared.

Occupation of household head (reference category=head without a job)

   (5) Manager or professional (yes $=1$).

   (6) Technical, sales, or administrative support (yes $=1$).

   (7) Service worker (yes $=1$).

   (8) Precision production, craft or repair (yes $=1$).

   (9) Operator, fabricator, or laborer (yes $=1$).

Metropolitan Area Characteristics

   (1) Fraction of metropolitan area labor force who are women over the age of 19 who have a high school education or less.

   (2) Metropolitan area unemployment rate.

   (3) Population of the metropolitan area.

   (4) Fraction of the metropolitan area population that is black.

   (5) Fraction of jobs in the metropolitan area that are in operator, fabricator, or laborer occupations.

   (6) Fraction of jobs in service occupations.

   (7) Fraction of jobs in sales occupations.

   (8) Fraction of jobs in clerical occupations.

   (9) Fraction of jobs in precision production, craft, or repair occupations.

---

centages, reported in tables 4.4 and 4.5, indicate the following for both male and female teenagers:

1. The enrollment rates of all groups rise with the level of family income, particularly in the case of older teenagers. Employment rates also rise with income, but the increases are smaller than they are for enrollment rates.
2. In comparison to younger teenagers, older teenagers are less frequently in the enrolled-not employed state and more frequently in the two nonenrolled states. As a result, employment rates are higher for older teenagers and enrollment rates are lower.
3. Younger blacks and Hispanics are less likely to be in the enrolled-employed state and more likely to be in the enrolled-not employed state in comparison to whites. Employment rates are therefore lower for younger minorities than younger whites, but enrollment rates are very similar among the races.
4. In comparison to older white teenagers, older blacks and Hispanics are less frequently in the enrolled-employed state, somewhat more frequently in the enrolled-not employed state, less frequently in the not enrolled-employed state, and much more frequently in the not enrolled-not employed state. Both employment and enrollment rates are lower for older minority teenagers than for older whites.

Regarding the magnitudes of the racial differences in employment and enrollment rates, the employment rates of whites are roughly twice as high as those for blacks, regardless of age or gender. The employment rate gaps between Hispanics and whites are roughly 40 percent as large as the black-white differences. Racial differences in enrollment rates are all small for younger teenagers, after controlling for family income level. Black-white differences in enrollment rates for older teenagers are small for youth in the two lowest income groups, but are 9 to 11 (5 to 9) percentage points lower for black males (females) in the two highest income groups. The enrollment rates for older Hispanics are noticeably lower than for whites or blacks, regardless of gender or family income level. For example, for youths with family incomes between $25,000

Table 4.4 Enrollment-Employment Outcomes of Male Teenagers
(Percentage of Sample in Each State)

	Enrolled-Employed	Enrolled Not Employed	Not Enrolled-Employed	Not Enrolled-Not Employed	Employed	Enrolled
Whites						
16–17 Years Old						
$Y1$[a]	25.5	57.9	5.1	11.5	30.6	83.4
$Y2$	33.3	58.9	3.9	3.9	37.2	92.2
$Y3$	36.9	57.7	2.0	3.4	38.9	94.6
$Y4$	37.6	58.8	1.8	1.9	39.4	96.4
18–19 Years Old						
$Y1$	22.9	26.2	28.2	22.8	51.1	49.1
$Y2$	32.2	31.5	22.1	14.3	54.3	63.7
$Y3$	38.8	33.6	16.3	11.3	55.1	72.4
$Y4$	41.2	40.5	12.2	6.1	53.4	81.7
Blacks						
16–17 Years Old						
$Y1$	11.1	78.2	2.0	8.8	13.1	89.3
$Y2$	14.9	77.2	1.0	6.6	15.9	92.1
$Y3$	18.4	76.2	1.0	4.6	19.4	94.6
$Y4$	16.3	78.2	1.8	3.6	18.1	94.5
18–19 Years Old						
$Y1$	11.9	41.0	14.4	32.7	26.3	52.9
$Y2$	16.1	45.4	13.7	24.8	29.8	61.5
$Y3$	21.3	42.0	13.7	23.0	35.0	63.3
$Y4$	21.0	49.7	11.5	17.7	32.5	70.7

Hispanics

16–17 Years Old

$Y1$	14.8	64.6	6.7	14.0	21.5	79.4
$Y2$	23.2	62.4	5.5	9.0	28.7	85.6
$Y3$	27.7	61.7	5.0	5.6	32.7	89.4
$Y4$	29.3	62.2	4.1	4.4	33.4	91.5

18–19 Years Old

$Y1$	12.0	30.1	26.7	30.6	38.7	42.1
$Y2$	17.8	30.2	30.4	21.6	48.2	48.0
$Y3$	21.4	35.4	28.4	14.9	49.8	56.8
$Y4$	26.6	37.9	21.1	14.5	47.7	64.5

[a] $Y1, \ldots Y4$ represent annual family income for the year 1979 net of the youth's earnings. $0 \leq Y1 \leq \$15,000$; $\$15,000 < Y2 \leq \$25,000$; $\$25,000 < Y3 \leq \$35,000$; $Y4 > \$35,000$.

Table 4.5 Enrollment-Employment Outcomes of Female Teenagers (Percentage of Sample in Each State)

	Enrolled-Employed	Enrolled Not Employed	Not Enrolled-Employed	Not Enrolled-Not Employed	Employed	Enrolled
Whites						
16–17 Years Old						
$Y1$[a]	27.5	57.8	3.6	11.1	31.1	85.3
$Y2$	32.3	61.5	1.8	4.4	34.1	93.8
$Y3$	37.0	58.9	1.9	2.2	38.9	95.9
$Y4$	36.8	61.2	1.0.	1.4	37.8	98.0
18–19 Years Old						
$Y1$	25.8	29.4	18.8	26.1	44.6	55.2
$Y2$	36.7	34.6	13.3	15.4	50.0	71.3
$Y3$	44.3	33.7	10.3	11.7	54.6	78.0
$Y4$	47.7	38.0	7.9	6.5	55.6	85.7
Blacks						
16–17 Years Old						
$Y1$	11.3	77.9	1.0	10.0	12.3	89.2
$Y2$	15.9	77.4	1.0	5.8	16.9	93.3
$Y3$	15.7	79.6	1.0	4.0	16.7	95.3
$Y4$	16.8	80.6	0.0	2.5	16.8	97.4
18–19 Years Old						
$Y1$	11.6	46.4	7.1	35.0	18.7	58.0
$Y2$	16.7	50.6	8.0	24.8	24.7	67.3
$Y3$	21.2	51.8	6.0	21.0	27.2	73.0
$Y4$	25.1	51.3	6.4	17.2	31.5	76.4

Hispanics

16–17 Years Old

$Y1$	14.3	68.3	3.6	13.8	17.9	82.6
$Y2$	18.2	70.0	3.1	8.6	21.3	88.2
$Y3$	25.5	63.5	3.0	8.0	28.5	89.0
$Y4$	26.9	66.2	3.0	4.0	29.9	93.1

18–19 Years Old

$Y1$	14.6	38.5	14.6	32.3	29.2	53.1
$Y2$	21.0	38.5	14.4	26.2	35.4	59.5
$Y3$	25.7	39.1	16.5	18.8	42.2	64.8
$Y4$	28.0	43.9	15.3	12.7	43.3	71.9

[a] $Y1,\dots Y4$ represent annual family income for the year 1979 net of the youth's earnings. $0 \le Y1 \le \$15,000$; $\$15,000 < Y2 \le \$25,000$; $\$25,000 < Y3 \le \$35,000$; $Y4 > \$35,000$.

and \$35,000, the enrollment rate for Hispanic males is 15.6 percentage points lower than for whites and 6.5 percentage points lower than for blacks. Similar differences exist for Hispanic females.

The Estimated Effects of Intraurban Job Accessibility

The estimated multinomial logit coefficients indicate the effect of a unit change in an independent variable on the log of the ratio of the probability of being in one of the first three enrollment-employment states to the probability of being in the fourth state (i.e., not enrolled-not employed). As such, these coefficients are cumbersome to interpret, particularly if the interest is in the effect of an independent variable on the sum of two probabilities, as it is in the present analysis. To provide a simpler method of presenting the multinomial logit results, I first computed the implied partial derivative of each probability with respect to a unit change in the independent variable at the mean values of the probabilities. I then used these estimates to determine how a five-minute reduction in travel time would affect the probability that the youth is in each of the four enrollment-employment states.

Five minutes was used as the hypothetical improvement in job access for the same reasons outlined in chapter 3. Results are presented in tables 4.6 and 4.7 for younger and older teenagers, respectively. These tables also give asymptotic t-statistics for each partial derivative as well as Wald test statistics. The latter statistics are distributed chi-squared and test the joint hypothesis that all of the logit coefficients associated with the travel time variable are zero. If this test statistic is significant, then the null hypothesis that job access does not affect the enrollment-employment decision can be rejected.[9]

Considering that 24 multinomial logit models were estimated — the 12 groups times the two job access measures — an overview of the results is warranted before proceeding to the individual tables. First, the estimated job access effects obtained with the two measures of travel time are similar in magnitude for all 12 groups. However, the mean travel times of workers in youth-intensive occupations provided the best fit for all of the younger teenager groups, while the mean times of low-wage workers performed best for all of the older teenager groups. An explanation for this difference is that older teenagers work in a greater variety of occupations than younger teenagers, which is better reflected in the construction of the measure of expected commuting time that is based on all low-wage jobs. The tables report the results obtained with the times based on youth-intensive jobs for younger teenagers and low-wage jobs for older teenagers.

Second, job access is found to have a strong effect on the job probability of all 12 groups, regardless of family income level. Third, the fact that job access is worse for minorities than for whites accounts for a significant portion of the differences in employment rates that exist between racial groups. Fourth, better job access is *not* found to reduce the school enrollment of any of the 12 groups of youths. Generally, it is found to have a neutral effect on the enrollment probabilities of younger teenagers and a positive effect on the enrollment probabilities of older teenagers. Finally, the effects of job access on the enrollment-employment outcomes tend to vary across groups in accordance with the theory presented in the second section of this chapter. I will now discuss the specific findings obtained for each of the groups.

The results for younger teenagers are very similar across the six race/sex groups (see table 4.6). The Wald test statistics are all significant at the 1 percent level, except for black females, where the levels of significance are somewhat lower. These results indicate that job access does affect the enrollment-employment state chosen by a teenager. For all groups, the principal effect of better job access is to increase the probability of the enrolled-employed state ($P1$) and to reduce the probability of the enrolled-not employed state ($P2$). The results are therefore consistent with the hypothesis that younger teenagers place a low value on current, relative to future, earnings and are therefore more likely to be on the margin between the two enrollment states.

For all of the younger groups, except black males, better job access has little effect on the probabilities of the two nonenrolled states ($P3$ and $P4$). The increase in $P1$ and reduction in $P2$ therefore results in a statistically significant increase in the probability of having a job ($P1+$

Table 4.6 Estimated Changes for Younger Teenagers in the Probability of Each Enrollment-Employment State from a Five-Minute Decrease in Expected Travel Time (Asymptotic t-Statistics)

	$P1$[a]	$P2$	$P3$	$P4$	Employed $(P1+P3)$	Enrolled $(P1+P2)$	χ^2
White Males							
$Y1$[b]	.070	−.060	−.005	−.005	.065	.010	11.90***
	(3.23)	(2.73)	(0.84)	(0.87)	(3.00)	(1.18)	
$Y2$	.070	−.065	−.005	.000	.070	.005	17.45***
	(4.42)	(4.31)	(0.59)	(0.33)	(4.30)	(0.63)	
$Y3$	.075	−.070	.005	−.005	.080	.005	20.48***
	(3.91)	(3.68)	(0.54)	(0.83)	(4.15)	(0.26)	
$Y4$	.075	−.070	−.005	−.005	.070	.010	17.77***
	(3.97)	(3.43)	(0.48)	(0.62)	(3.75)	(0.78)	
Black Males							
$Y1$	.055	−.040	−.005	−.010	.055	.015	51.54***
	(9.57)	(4.92)	(1.51)	(1.74)	(8.05)	(2.20)	
$Y2$	.055	−.040	.000	−.015	.055	.015	51.96***
	(9.63)	(4.74)	(0.39)	(2.16)	(7.85)	(2.08)	
$Y3$	.050	−.060	.000	−.015	.050	.010	38.13***
	(5.15)	(3.00)	(0.31)	(1.82)	(4.93)	(1.49)	
$Y4$	.050	−.040	.000	−.010	.050	.010	27.51***
	(6.12)	(3.78)	(0.10)	(1.09)	(5.75)	(1.04)	
Hispanic Males							
$Y1$	.045	−.040	−.005	.000	.040	.010	17.01***
	(5.31)	(3.52)	(0.78)	(0.23)	(4.18)	(0.67)	
$Y2$	.050	−.040	−.005	−.005	.045	.010	19.30***
	(5.45)	(3.04)	(0.69)	(0.35)	(4.48)	(0.69)	
$Y3$	.050	−.040	−.010	.000	.040	.005	18.95***
	(3.49)	(2.42)	(1.06)	(0.11)	(2.65)	(0.57)	
$Y4$	.035	−.030	.000	.010	.040	.005	16.41***
	(2.69)	(2.06)	(0.61)	(0.85)	(2.94)	(0.55)	
White Females							
$Y1$	.055	−.050	.010	−.015	.065	.005	14.98***
	(2.46)	(2.24)	(1.22)	(1.95)	(2.84)	(0.59)	
$Y2$	.055	−.055	.010	−.010	.070	.000	21.37***
	(2.95)	(2.94)	(2.53)	(1.50)	(3.52)	(0.09)	
$Y3$	.050	−.055	.010	−.005	.060	.000	16.77***
	(4.37)	(4.60)	(2.15)	(0.95)	(5.22)	(0.31)	
$Y4$	.050	−.050	.010	−.010	.060	.000	14.70***
	(2.78)	(2.58)	(1.72)	(1.25)	(3.14)	(0.13)	

Table 4.6 (*continued*)

	$P1$[a]	$P2$	$P3$	$P4$	Employed $(P1+P3)$	Enrolled $(P1+P2)$	χ^2
Black Females							
$Y1$	.020	−.010	−.005	−.005	.015	.010	7.47*
	(2.31)	(0.85)	(1.48)	(0.89)	(1.79)	(1.33)	
$Y2$	.025	−.015	−.005	−.005	.020	.010	10.11**
	(2.75)	(1.36)	(1.73)	(0.62)	(2.14)	(1.16)	
$Y3$	.030	−.025	−.005	−.005	.025	.010	13.74***
	(2.61)	(1.50)	(1.72)	(0.29)	(2.00)	(0.78)	
$Y4$	.030	−.025	−.005	.000	.025	.005	8.40**
	(2.71)	(1.98)	(0.75)	(0.07)	(2.26)	(0.30)	
Hispanic Females							
$Y1$	.040	−.025	−.010	−.005	.030	.015	14.89***
	(3.56)	(2.06)	(1.72)	(0.48)	(2.62)	(1.29)	
$Y2$	.045	−.035	−.010	−.005	.040	.015	21.04***
	(4.21)	(2.74)	(1.55)	(0.51)	(3.39)	(1.20)	
$Y3$	.040	−.020	−.010	−.010	.035	.020	15.40***
	(5.12)	(1.95)	(1.55)	(1.08)	(3.72)	(1.68)	
$Y4$	.045	−.025	−.010	−.015	.035	.025	15.31***
	(5.61)	(1.36)	(1.60)	(1.02)	(2.62)	(1.06)	

[a] $P1$ = Enrolled-Employed, $P2$ = Enrolled-Not Employed, $P3$ = Not Enrolled-Employed, $P4$ = Not Enrolled-Not Employed.

[b] $Y1, \ldots Y4$ represent annual family income for the year 1979 net of the youth's earnings. $0 \le Y1 \le \$15,000$; $\$15,000 < Y2 \le \$25,000$; $\$25,000 < Y3 \le \$35,000$; $Y4 > \$35,000$.

The χ^2 statistics reported in the last column are for a Wald test, which indicates whether the travel-time variable has a statistically significant effect on the enrollment-employment state. *** and ** and * indicate significance at the 1 percent, 5 percent, and 10 percent levels, respectively.

$P3$), but school enrollment ($P1 + P2$) is not affected. These same results were obtained for black males in the highest family income group. For black males in the other income groups, the increase in $P1$ and reduction in $P2$ is accompanied by a statistically significant decrease, albeit small, in the probability of the not enrolled-not employed state ($P4$). As a result, better job access has a positive effect on both the probability of employment and enrollment for most younger black male teenagers.

In contrast to the similarity in the results for younger teenagers, the results for older teenagers (see table 4.7) are generally different across

Table 4.7 Estimated Changes for Older Teenagers in the Probability of Each Enrollment-Employment State from a Five-Minute Decrease in Expected Travel Time (Asymptotic t-Statistics)

	$P1$[a]	$P2$	$P3$	$P4$	Employed $(P1+P3)$	Enrolled $(P1+P2)$	χ^2
White Males							
$Y1$[b]	.045	.015	−.005	−.055	.035	.060	12.33***
	(1.81)	(0.63)	(0.37)	(3.49)	(1.54)	(2.30)	
$Y2$	.050	−.005	.000	−.045	.050	.045	13.08***
	(2.46)	(0.25)	(0.05)	(3.20)	(2.57)	(1.92)	
$Y3$	.050	−.010	.010	−.050	.060	.040	14.45***
	(2.45)	(0.54)	(0.43)	(3.29)	(2.89)	(1.61)	
$Y4$	.050	−.020	.005	−.040	.060	.030	10.07**
	(2.13)	(0.88)	(0.32)	(2.41)	(2.56)	(1.23)	
Black Males							
$Y1$	.040	.020	.005	−.060	.045	.055	27.57***
	(5.09)	(1.40)	(0.49)	(4.46)	(4.44)	(3.45)	
$Y2$	.035	.015	.005	−.055	.040	.050	23.84***
	(4.84)	(1.04)	(0.52)	(4.02)	(4.27)	(3.06)	
$Y3$	.035	.025	.000	−.060	.035	.055	21.43***
	(3.37)	(1.83)	(0.09)	(4.22)	(2.84)	(3.39)	
$Y4$	.040	.005	.000	−.045	.040	.050	17.42***
	(3.97)	(0.47)	(0.02)	(2.95)	(2.82)	(2.86)	
Hispanic Males							
$Y1$	.040	−.030	.000	−.010	.040	.010	8.54**
	(2.67)	(1.36)	(0.06)	(0.64)	(1.79)	(0.44)	
$Y2$	.040	−.025	.000	−.015	.040	.010	9.42**
	(2.74)	(1.30)	(0.12)	(0.85)	(1.89)	(0.55)	
$Y3$	.040	−.035	.005	−.005	.040	.000	9.08**
	(2.45)	(1.79)	(0.17)	(0.23)	(1.97)	(0.03)	
$Y4$	.040	−.030	.000	−.010	.040	.010	6.39*
	(2.20)	(1.29)	(0.03)	(0.51)	(1.65)	(0.38)	
White Females							
$Y1$	.075	−.040	−.020	−.020	.060	.040	11.46***
	(3.45)	(1.84)	(1.37)	(1.19)	(2.72)	(1.72)	
$Y2$	.095	−.050	−.020	−.025	.075	.045	21.32***
	(4.35)	(2.44)	(1.51)	(1.68)	(3.59)	(2.23)	
$Y3$	.101	−.050	−.020	−.030	.090	.050	23.60***
	(5.62)	(3.08)	(1.60)	(1.79)	(4.79)	(2.32)	
$Y4$	.100	−.050	−.025	−.020	.075	.050	22.46***
	(5.58)	(3.13)	(1.85)	(1.32)	(4.32)	(2.18)	

Table 4.7 (*continued*)

	$P1$[a]	$P2$	$P3$	$P4$	Employed $(P1+P3)$	Enrolled $(P1+P2)$	χ^2
Black Females							
$Y1$	.025	−.030	.010	−.010	.040	−.005	9.82**
	(2.21)	(1.58)	(1.39)	(0.60)	(2.85)	(0.12)	
$Y2$	.020	−.030	.010	.000	.030	−.010	7.44*
	(2.17)	(1.71)	(1.17)	(0.02)	(2.33)	(0.52)	
$Y3$	.015	−.035	.015	.010	.030	−.025	6.58*
	(1.05)	(2.03)	(1.78)	(0.48)	(1.87)	(1.33)	
$Y4$	.005	−.045	.015	.025	.020	−.040	5.69
	(0.32)	(2.21)	(1.73)	(1.14)	(1.28)	(1.92)	
Hispanic Females							
$Y1$	.040	−.005	.015	−.050	.050	.035	6.33*
	(1.92)	(0.13)	(0.71)	(1.95)	(2.22)	(1.17)	
$Y2$	.040	.005	.010	−.055	.050	.045	7.30*
	(2.18)	(0.13)	(0.60)	(2.22)	(2.31)	(1.48)	
$Y3$	.035	.005	.000	−.045	.040	.045	4.79
	(1.72)	(0.25)	(0.12)	(1.78)	(1.56)	(1.49)	
$Y4$	.045	−.010	.000	−.030	.045	.035	4.19
	(2.09)	(0.38)	(0.11)	(1.01)	(1.64)	(1.01)	

[a] $P1$ = Enrolled-Employed, $P2$ = Enrolled-Not Employed, $P3$ = Not Enrolled-Employed, $P4$ = Not Enrolled-Not Employed.

[b] $Y1,\ldots Y4$ represent annual family income for the year 1979 net of the youth's earnings. $0 \le Y1 \le \$15,000$; $\$15,000 < Y2 \le \$25,000$; $\$25,000 < Y3 \le \$35,000$; $Y4 > \$35,000$.

The χ^2 statistics reported in the last column are for a Wald test, which indicates whether the travel-time variable has a statistically significant effect on the enrollment-employment state. *** and ** and * indicate significance at the 1 percent, 5 percent, and 10 percent levels, respectively.

the various groups. An exception to this are the results obtained for white and black males. These results are considered first. Regardless of the level of family income, the Wald test statistics indicate that job access has a highly significant effect on the chosen enrollment-employment state of both white and black males. For both groups, better job access is found to increase the probability of the enrolled-employed state, decrease the probability of the not enrolled-not employed state, and leave unaffected the probabilities of the states in between. As a result, there is a higher probability of having a job and a higher probability of school enrollment. The employment and enrollment effects are generally significant at the 1 percent level. For whites, but not for blacks, the magnitude of the school enrollment effect is found to vary inversely with the level of family income. These results lend support to the hypothesis that teenagers from families with higher family income are less likely to place a relatively high value on current earnings. The contrary findings for blacks may reflect the fact that at the same level of measured annual income, black families have less wealth, greater income instability, and more members than white families; hence, even within the higher income groups, black teenagers may have a strong desire for current earnings.

The results obtained for older Hispanic male teenagers are quite different from those obtained for whites and blacks. Older Hispanic males are found to be affected by job access in the same manner as their younger counterparts; that is, better job access increases their employment but not their school enrollment. I can offer no theoretical explanation for the difference in results between older Hispanic males and the other groups of older male teenagers; however, the Wald test statistics and the t-statistics on individual effects are lower for Hispanic males than for the other groups. This suggests that the anomalous results obtained for Hispanic males may be a statistical artifact. Recall that the sample sizes of older Hispanics are less than half the size of those employed for the other groups. In addition, as suggested in chapter 3, there is possibly greater measurement error in the travel time variables computed for Hispanics, since their construction was based on much smaller samples than those available for whites and blacks.

Turning now to the results obtained for older female teenagers, consider first those for whites. As was true for white and black males, better job access increases the probability of the enrolled-employed state and decreases the probability of the not enrolled-not employed state; however, the declines in the latter probability are smaller than those observed for older males. In addition, there are statistically significant declines in the enrolled-not employed state for females that were not in evidence for males. These results are consistent with the hypothesis that females, in comparison to males, are more likely to be on the margin between the two enrollment states, because they place less value on current, in comparison to future, earnings. There is also a tendency for the probability of the not enrolled-employed state to decline with better job access. These changes from better job access in the probabilities of the enrollment-employment states for older white females result in statistically significant and positive employment and enrollment effects for all four income groups.

The Wald test statistics are relatively low for older black female teenagers, and in the case of the highest income group the statistic is not significant at even the 10 percent level. The results for older black females parallel those obtained for younger black females. Better job access increases the probability of the enrolled-employed state, decreases the probability of the enrolled-not employed state, and has little effect on the two non-enrollment states. The failure to observe a positive school enrollment effect for older black females may be the result of child-rearing responsibilities. Fifty-two percent of the older black females in the not enrolled-not employed state have borne a child. In contrast, 29 percent of the white females in this state have borne a child. Hence, black females are less likely to be on the margin between the enrolled-employed and not enrolled-not employed states.

Older Hispanic female teenagers are affected by better job access in a manner similar to that observed for white females, in that both school enrollment and employment are found to increase. While the magnitudes of the estimated job access effects are similar to those obtained for the other groups where a positive school enrollment effect is observed, the Wald test statistics and the t-statistics on individual partial derivatives are frequently not significant at conventional levels. As noted above, the lower levels of significance for older Hispanic teenagers may reflect smaller sample sizes and greater imprecision in the measurement of the travel-time variable.

Thus far the analysis has focused on the statistical significance of the changes in enrollment-employment probabilities resulting from an improvement in the teenager's access to jobs. To better gauge the economic significance of the results, consider the percentage changes in job and enrollment probabilities from a five-minute reduction in travel time. The percentage changes are calculated at the mean values of the probabilities (see tables 4.8 and 4.9). For all 12 groups, a five-minute reduction in time would cause large percentage increases in the probability of the enrolled-employed state (column 1) and in the probability of having a job (column 5). For most older teenagers there would also be a substantial decline in the probability of the not enrolled-not employed state.

Perhaps the results of greatest interest are those pertaining to central city black males. The low employment and enrollment rates of these youths have become one of the most serious social concerns confronting policymakers. Roughly 90 percent of all inner city black teenagers are in the lowest two income groups included in my analysis (i.e., family income of less than $25,000). For younger black male teenagers in these income groups, a five-minute reduction in travel time would increase the probability of having a job by 35 percent and increase the probability of school enrollment by 2 percent. For older teenagers, there would be a 15 percent increase in job probability and a 10 percent increase in the school enrollment rate.

The economic significance of the estimated job access effects is also revealed by determining the role that access plays in explaining racial differences in employment and enrollment rates. The most interesting case to consider is that of older black male teenagers. The strong effects of job access on the employment and enrollment probabilities of this group, combined with the fact that they possess relatively poor access to jobs (see table 4.2), suggest that job access may account for a sizeable portion of their lower employment and enrollment rates in comparison to whites. Table 4.4 indicates that both employment and enrollment rates are substantially lower for blacks than whites in the $25,000 to $35,000 family income group. To what extent can these differentials be attributed to the fact that blacks have inferior access to jobs? To determine this, two pseudo-experiments were conducted. Essentially, the experiments involved randomly allocating the white (black) travel times to blacks (whites) so that the resulting frequency distribution of travel times for blacks (whites) is the same as it originally was for whites (blacks).

Using the multinomial logit equation for blacks (whites), the employ-

Table 4.8 Percentage Changes in the Enrollment-Employment Outcomes of Younger Teenagers Caused by a Five-Minute Reduction in Expected Travel Time

	$P1$[a]	$P2$	$P3$	$P4$	Employed $(P1+P3)$	Enrolled $(P1+P2)$
White Males						
$Y1$[b]	27***	−10***	−10	−4	21***	1
$Y2$	21***	−11***	−12	0	19***	1
$Y3$	20***	−12***	25	−15	21***	1
$Y4$	20***	−12***	−28	−26	18***	1
Black Males						
$Y1$	49***	−5***	−25	−11*	42***	2**
$Y2$	37***	−5***	0	−23**	34***	2**
$Y3$	27***	−5***	0	−32*	26***	1
$Y4$	31***	−5***	0	−27	28***	1
Hispanic Males						
$Y1$	30***	−6***	−7	0	19***	1
$Y2$	22***	−6***	−9	−5	16***	1
$Y3$	18***	−6**	−20	0	12***	1
$Y4$	12***	−5**	0	22	12***	1
White Females						
$Y1$	20***	−9**	27	−14**	21***	0
$Y2$	17***	−9***	55**	−23	21***	0
$Y3$	13***	9***	52**	−22	15***	0
$Y4$	14***	−8***	100*	−357	16***	0
Black Females						
$Y1$	18**	−1	−50	−5	12*	1
$Y2$	16***	−2	−50*	−9	12**	1
$Y3$	19***	−3	−50*	−12	15**	1
$Y4$	18***	−3**	0	0	15**	1
Hispanic Females						
$Y1$	28***	−4**	−28*	−4	17***	2
$Y2$	25***	−5***	−32	−6	19***	2
$Y3$	16***	−3*	−33	−12	12***	2*
$Y4$	17***	−4	−33	−37	12***	3

NOTE: Percentage changes are calculated at the mean values of the probabilities.

[a] $P1$ = Enrolled-Employed, $P2$ = Enrolled-Not Employed, $P3$ = Not Enrolled-Employed, $P4$ = Not Enrolled-Not Employed.

[b] $Y1, \ldots Y4$ represent annual family income for the year 1979 net of the youth's earnings. $0 \le Y1 \le \$15,000$; $\$15,000 < Y2 \le \$25,000$; $\$25,000 < Y3 \le \$35,000$; $Y4 > \$35,000$.

*** and ** and * indicate that the implied partial derivative is significant by a two-tailed test at the 1 percent, 5 percent, and 10 percent levels, respectively.

Table 4.9 Percentage Changes in the Enrollment-Employment Outcomes of Older Teenagers Caused by a Five-Minute Reduction in Expected Travel Time

	$P1$[a]	$P2$	$P3$	$P4$	Employed $(P1+P3)$	Enrolled $(P1+P2)$
White Males						
$Y1$[b]	20*	6	−2	−24***	7	12**
$Y2$	16**	−2	0	−31***	9***	7*
$Y3$	13**	−3	6	−44***	11***	6
$Y4$	12**	−5	4	−65**	11***	4
Black Males						
$Y1$	34***	5	3	−18***	17***	10***
$Y2$	22***	3	4	−22***	13***	8***
$Y3$	16***	6*	0	−26***	15***	9***
$Y4$	19***	1	0	−25***	12***	7***
Hispanic Males						
$Y1$	33***	−10	0	−3	10*	2
$Y2$	22***	−8	0	−7	8	2
$Y3$	19**	−10*	2	−3	8**	1
$Y4$	15**	−8	0	−7	8*	1
White Females						
$Y1$	29***	−14*	−11	−8	−13***	7*
$Y2$	26***	−14**	−15	−16*	15***	6**
$Y3$	23***	−15***	−19	−26*	15***	6**
$Y4$	21***	−13***	−32*	−31	13***	6**
Black Females						
$Y1$	22**	−6	14	−3	21***	−1
$Y2$	12**	−6*	12	0	12**	−1
$Y3$	7	−7**	25*	5	11*	−3
$Y4$	2	−9**	23*	15	6	−5*
Hispanic Females						
$Y1$	27*	1	10	−15*	17*	7
$Y2$	19***	−1	7	−21**	14**	8
$Y3$	14**	−1*	0	−24*	9**	7
$Y4$	16**	2	0	−24	10*	5

NOTE: Percentage changes are calculated at the mean values of the probabilities.

[a] $P1$ = Enrolled-Employed, $P2$ = Enrolled-Not Employed, $P3$ = Not Enrolled-Employed, $P4$ = Not Enrolled-Not Employed.

[b] $Y1,\ldots Y4$ represent annual family income for the year 1979 net of the youth's earnings. $0 \le Y1 \le \$15,000$; $\$15,000 < Y2 \le \$25,000$; $\$25,000 < Y3 \le \$35,000$; $Y4 > \$35,000$.

*** and ** and * indicate that the implied partial derivative is significant by a two-tailed test at the 1 percent, 5 percent, and 10 percent levels, respectively.

ment probability ($P1 + P3$) and the school enrollment probability ($P1 + P2$) were calculated for each black (white) teenager, taking into account the travel time each black (white) had been allocated. The means of these probabilities serve as the hypothetical employment and enrollment rates blacks (whites) would have if they had the same access to jobs as whites (blacks). The hypothetical rate of employment for blacks (whites) was subtracted from the actual rate of employment for whites (blacks) to determine the employment rate difference that would exist if blacks and whites had the same access to jobs. This predicted difference in employment rates was subtracted from the actual difference in employment rates and expressed as a percentage of the actual difference. The results of the two experiments may differ, because the coefficients from the black (white) youth logit equation are used with the white (black) travel times. The same procedures were followed to determine the percentage of the gap in school enrollment rates attributable to differences in job access.

Allocating the white times to blacks explains 35 percent and 46 percent of the racial differences in employment and school enrollment rates, respectively. Allocating the black times to whites explains 37 percent and 25 percent of these same differences. Clearly, job access is important in explaining differences in both school enrollment and employment between the groups.

Results Obtained with the Control Variables

The estimated changes in the probabilities of each of the four enrollment/employment states that would result from a unit change in each of the metropolitan area variables (i.e., the implied partial derivatives) are reported in the appendix to this chapter. The results are generally consistent with those obtained from estimating the job probability equations described in the sixth section of chapter 3. The following variables yielded noteworthy results: (1) the fraction of the metropolitan population who are black; (2) the fraction of the metropolitan area labor force who are women over the age of 19 who have a high school education or less; (3) the metropolitan area unemployment rate; and (4) the set of variables indicating the fraction of the metropolitan area's jobs in each of five youth-intensive occupational groups.

The fraction of the metropolitan population who are black has a significant effect on the enrollment/employment state of whites but has little effect on minorities. For whites of both sex and age groups, an increase in the fraction of black population increases the probability of the enrolled-employed state and decreases the probability of the enrolled-not employed state. As a result, the probability of having a job is higher for white teenagers living in metropolitan areas with larger black populations. As mentioned in chapter 3, this suggests that whites encounter less competition for jobs from blacks than they do from other whites. This could reflect the possibility that blacks are relatively less qualified, or that employers prefer to hire whites over blacks for prejudicial reasons.

The Wald test statistics indicate that the fraction of the metropolitan area labor force who are women over the age of 19 who have a high school education or less has a highly significant effect on the enrollment/ employment states of white teenagers, regardless of age or gender. An increase in this variable decreases the probability of the enrolled-employed state and increases the probability of the enrolled-not employed state, thereby resulting in the white teenager having a lower employment probability. In contrast, the Wald test statistics are all insignificant for blacks and Hispanics. These results are consistent with those reported in chapter 3 and suggest that employers view less-educated adult females and white teenagers as closer substitutes for one another in making the hiring decision than they do adult females and minority teenagers.

In chapter 1, I pointed out that in their review of the research on the black youth employment crisis sponsored by the National Bureau of Economic Research, Freeman and Holzer (1986) concluded that a major determinant of black youth joblessness was the fraction of the labor force represented by women. This conclusion was based primarily on the work of Borjas (1986), who estimated wage and labor force participation equations for 18 to 24-year-old black males. Unfortunately, equations for black female youths or white youths were not estimated. Borjas' results are not necessarily inconsistent with mine, since we focus on youths in different age groups. It is likely to be true that adult women and older black male youths are more competitive in the labor market than adult women and black teenagers, especially those who are not high school graduates. While this issue lies beyond the scope of the present study, it certainly deserves attention in future work.

The Wald test statistics indicate that the metropolitan area unemployment rate has a significant effect on the enrollment/employment states of all 12 groups of teenagers. A tighter labor market, as measured by a decrease in the unemployment rate, increases the expected earnings, and therefore utilities, associated with the enrolled-employed state as well as the not enrolled-employed state. The probability of having a job is, therefore, expected to rise, but the effect on school enrollment is ambiguous. The results indicate that a decrease in the unemployment rate increases the employment probabilities of all 12 groups and that all of the effects are highly significant.

The magnitudes of these effects are similar among the various groups. The unemployment rate is found to have a statistically significant effect on the probability of school enrollment for only two groups: younger white male and younger Hispanic male teenagers. For these groups, a decrease in the unemployment rate is found to decrease school enrollment, but the magnitude of the effects is quite small. For both groups, a 1 percentage point decrease in the unemployment rate reduces the probability of school enrollment by about 1 percentage point. The results obtained with the unemployment rate variable are of considerable interest, for they suggest that national or local policies designed to stimulate the level of aggregate demand will have desirable effects on youth employment without inducing high school students to drop out of school.[10]

The variables that measure the fraction of the metropolitan area's jobs in particular occupational categories yielded generally mixed results across the groups of teenagers. The fraction of jobs in the operatives category is found to have a positive and statistically significant effect on the employment probabilities of only younger and older white male teenagers. These effects are the result of an increase in the probability of the enrolled-employed state and a decline in the probability of the enrolled-not employed state. An increase in this variable is also found to reduce the school enrollment probabilities of older Hispanic and black female teenagers. Apparently for these groups, jobs in the operatives category are sufficiently attractive to induce youths to drop out of school.

The relative number of clerical jobs has little effect on the probabilities of the various groups. The fraction of jobs in service occupations is found to have a significant effect on the enrollment/employment states of young white males and females and older black males and females. For whites, an increase in this fraction increases the probability of the enrolled-employed state, thereby resulting in a positive effect on the probability of having a job. For blacks, an increase in service jobs increases the probability of the two enrollment states and decreases the probability of the two nonenrollment states, which results in a higher probability of school enrollment. These results suggest that enrolled black teenagers are dependent on jobs in service occupations, and if these jobs are scarce these youth are forced to drop out of school for economic reasons.

The Wald test statistics for the fraction of jobs in craft occupations are significant for older male and female blacks, younger male and female Hispanics, and younger white females. For blacks, an increase in this variable increases the probability of both employment and school enrollment. These effects are the result of an increase in the probability of the enrolled-employed state and a decrease in the probability of the not enrolled-not employed state. In contrast, an increase in craft jobs reduces the probability of school enrollment for Hispanics, but has little effect on the probability of having a job. The decline in school enrollment for Hispanic females is due to a reduction in the probability of the enrolled-not employed state and an increase in the probability of the not enrolled-not employed state. For Hispanic males, the lower school enrollment is the result of a decline in the probability of the enrolled-employed state and an increase in the not enrolled-not employed state. An increase in craft jobs also reduces the school enrollment probability of younger white female teenagers. But for them, there is a decrease in the enrolled-not employed state and an increase in the not enrolled-employed state. These results suggest that while an increase in the fraction of jobs in precision production, craft, and repair occupations influences both Hispanics and younger white females to drop out of school, white females have greater success in obtaining these jobs.

Perhaps the most interesting results obtained with the occupation variables are those for the fraction of jobs in sales occupations. For older blacks and older whites of both sexes, an increase in the relative number of these jobs is found to reduce the probability of school enrollment. All of the effects are highly significant. The reduction in school enrollment for these groups is due to a decrease in the probability of both of the enrolled states and an increase in the probability of both of the non-enrolled states. These results suggest that white and black teenagers find working in a sales occupation an attractive alternative to remaining in high school.

The other control variables included in the multinomial logit models are those that describe the characteristics of the individual youth and his/her family. The effects of these variables on the enrollment/employment probabilities are very similar across the different groups. These effects are illustrated in table 4.10, which reports the results for one of the groups, namely, younger white female teenagers. The following variables are found to have a statistically significant effect on the enrollment/employment state selected by the teenager: age, years of school, presence of a spouse in the household, health of the young woman, parenthood status, and occupational status and educational level of the family head of household. Older youths have a lower probability of being in the enrolled-not employed state and higher probabilities of being in the other three states. As the result of these changes, they have a higher probability of having a job and a lower probability of school enrollment. An increase in the number of years of school completed increases the probability of the enrolled-employed state and decreases the probability of the other three states, which results in an increase in both the probability of employment and enrollment.

The latter effect indicates that a young woman who is behind in grade

Table 4.10 Implied Partial Derivatives for Individual and Family Variables: White Females, 16–17 Years Old
(Asymptotic t-Statistics)

	$P1$[a]	$P2$	$P3$	$P4$	Employed $(P1+P3)$	Enrolled $(P1+P2)$	χ^2
Age	.0748	−.1466	.0224	.0494	.0972	−.0718	65.75***
	(5.01)	(9.41)	(5.15)	(8.53)	(6.42)	(10.60)	
Years of school	.0912	−.0410	−.0105	−.0397	.0807	.0502	201.20***
	(11.42)	(4.93)	(4.84)	(12.84)	(9.97)	(13.92)	
Spouse present	−.1903	−.1553	.1591	.1865	−.0313	−.3457	32.24***
	(2.32)	(1.82)	(7.14)	(5.87)	(0.38)	(9.29)	
Healthy	.1272	−.1083	.0283	−.0472	.1554	.0189	9.10**
	(2.41)	(1.97)	(1.97)	(2.31)	(2.91)	(0.79)	
Borne a child	−.1027	−.2112	.0263	.2876	−.0764	−.3140	32.34***
	(1.65)	(3.26)	(1.56)	(11.90)	(1.21)	(11.13)	
Female head	.0195	−.0171	.0014	−.0004	.0210	.0024	1.04
	(0.87)	(0.73)	(0.23)	(0.45)	(0.92)	(0.24)	
Education of head	.0017	.0094	−.0072	−.0040	−.0054	.0111	37.89***
	(0.72)	(3.88)	(4.41)	(2.56)	(2.12)	(6.12)	
Family income	.4572E-5	−.2508E-5	−.1153E-6	−.1949E-5	.4456E-5	.2064E-5	3.82
	(1.47)	(0.77)	(0.14)	(1.62)	(1.41)	(1.46)	
Family income squared	−6265E-10	.4464E-10	−.1036E-11	.1904E-10	−.6368E-10	−.1800E-10	5.99
	(2.09)	(1.43)	(0.13)	(1.64)	(2.10)	(1.33)	

Occupation of head (reference category is head without a job)

Manager or professional	.0427	−.0047	−.0053	−.0326	.0374	.0400	10.36**
	(1.57)	(0.17)	(0.72)	(3.09)	(1.35)	(3.07)	
Technical, sales, or administrative support	.0467	−.0112	.0032	−.0390	.0499	.0354	6.44*
	(1.79)	(0.41)	(0.45)	(3.83)	(1.89)	(3.00)	
Service worker	.0565	−.0382	.0106	−.0290	.0672	.0183	4.48
	(1.67)	(1.08)	(1.15)	(2.21)	(1.95)	(1.19)	
Craftsman	.0515	−.0046	.0002	−.0472	.0518	.0469	9.46**
	(1.91)	(0.16)	(0.03)	(4.50)	(1.89)	(3.83)	
Laborer	.0386	−.0352	.0183	−.0217	.0569	.0034	6.02
	(1.34)	(1.17)	(2.39)	(1.94)	(1.94)	(0.26)	

[a] $P1$ = Enrolled-Employed, $P2$ = Enrolled-Not Employed, $P3$ = Not Enrolled-Employed, $P4$ = Not Enrolled-Not Employed.

The χ^2 statistics reported in the last column are for a Wald test, which indicates whether the travel-time variable has a statistically significant effect on the enrollment-employment state. *** and ** and * indicate significance at the 1 percent, 5 percent, and 10 percent levels, respectively.

level for her age group has a higher probability of dropping out of high school. If she has a spouse, the probabilities of the two enrollment states are lower and the probabilities of the two nonenrollment states are higher. The net effect of these changes is that the probability of employment is unaffected but the probability of school enrollment is lower. If the youth has no mental or physical problems limiting the type of work she can perform, she is more likely to be in one of the employment states; hence, the probability of having a job is higher and there is no effect on school enrollment.

If the teenager has borne a child, the probabilities of the two enrollment states are lower, the probability of the not enrolled-not employed state is higher, and therefore the probability of school enrollment is lower. Teenagers with more highly educated family heads have a higher probability of being in the enrolled-not employed state and lower probabilities of being in the two nonenrollment states; therefore, the probability of employment is lower and the probability of school enrollment is higher. Finally, if the head of the household works in a more highly paid occupation (e.g., managerial, professional, or technical) the probabilities of employment and enrollment are both higher. This is due to the fact that the probability of the enrolled-employed state is higher and the probability of the not enrolled-not employed state is lower.

Conclusions

The primary objectives of the multinomial logit analysis presented in this chapter were to determine (1) the effect of intraurban job accessibility on the teenager's probability of having a job, when employment and school enrollment are treated as jointly endogenous variables, and (2) the probability of school enrollment being reduced by the teenager's proximity to jobs that he/she would be qualified to hold. The results strongly reinforce the conclusion reached in the previous chapter that job access has a strong effect on youth employment. They also reveal that better job access does not increase a teenager's probability of dropping out of high school and frequently results in higher school enrollment rates. Obviously, these results have important implications for public policy, which is the subject of the following chapter.

NOTES

[1] Recall from chapter 2 that exogenous means that the values of the variable are not explained by the model, but are given or provided from outside the model. Variables whose values are explained by the model are labeled endogenous.

[2] The higher labor force participation rates of older and male teenagers are only suggestive of a higher preference for work, because labor force participation rates are also a function of the set of employment opportunities available.

[3] Casual observation also supports the hypotheses that older and male teenagers are more desirous of current earnings. Older youths have a greater need to assert their independence from their parents, which a job enables them to do. Male youths have a greater need for income than female youths, because dating is more expensive for males.

[4] Samples 1 and 2 could not be used to conduct the analysis of this chapter, because they include teenagers who are high school graduates.

[5] Since the analysis is restricted to youths who have not graduated from high school, it may appear that the 18 to 19-year-old samples consist only of 'losers' (i.e., dropouts or enrolled youths overage for their grade). Approximately 50 percent of all 18 to 19-year-olds had not graduated from high school at the time the census was taken. About half of these people were dropouts and half were still in school. Of those in school, close to 90 percent were 18 years olds and information on their birth dates suggested that most were not overage for their grade.

[6] The only difference in the set of family and individual variables entering the multinomial logit equations — in comparison to the set used in chapter 3 to estimate the job probability equations — is that the nonlinear effect of family income was measured by including income and income squared rather than a set of income category dummy variables. In the case of the multinomial logit equations, the quadratic income specification provided superior fits.

[7] The decision to use metropolitan area descriptors rather than metropolitan area dummy variables was based on cost considerations. In the one case where the multinomial logit equation was alternatively estimated with dummies and descriptors, CPU time was 500 percent greater in the former case. The estimated job access effects were virtually identical between the two runs.

The metropolitan area variables entering the multinomial logit equations are identical to those described in chapter 3, except that variables indicating the fraction of the metropolitan area jobs in each of five separate occupational categories frequently containing youths were included (see table 4.3), instead of a single composite measure of the presence of lower-skills jobs in the metropolitan area. This change was made since the enrollment-employment decisions of teenagers were found to be differentially affected by the fraction of jobs in each occupational category.

[8] A number of independent variables not listed in table 4.3 were also tried. Like travel time, these variables were measured for the residential zone. They included the mean educational level of the male population over the age of 25, the percentage of workers in the zone who use public transit to get to work, the percentage of the population who are black, and the percentage of the population who are below the poverty line. These variables were generally not significant and their inclusion had little effect on the results obtained with travel time. They were, therefore, not included in the final runs.

[9] Also computed were two specification-error test statistics. The first tested for the independence from irrelevant alternatives property (IIA) of the multinomial logit model (Hausman and McFadden 1984). The IIA property, which states the ratio of the probabilities of choosing any two alternatives is the same irrespective of the total number of choices considered, is a potentially serious shortcoming of the logit model. The Hausman-McFadden test statistic for the IIA property is:

$$T = (\theta_A - \theta_C)'[\mathrm{cov}(\theta_A) - \mathrm{cov}(\theta_C)]^{-1}(\theta_A - \theta_C),$$

where C is the full choice set and A is a proper subset of C. θ represents the maximum likelihood estimators and $\mathrm{cov}(\theta)$ the estimated asymptotic covariance matrices. Under the null hypothesis that the IIA property holds, $\theta_A - \theta_C$ is a consistent estimator of zero. For selected subgroups, T was computed four times, alternatively dropping each of the four choices to form the A subset. In no case did T come close to any reasonable critical value for a χ^2 test. The hypothesis that the IIA property holds was therefore not rejected.

The second test statistic was the F-test suggested by Moulton and Randolph (1989) to test for the presence of error components arising from the use of aggregate variables in micro equations (see chapter 3, footnote 5). To conduct this test, multiple outcome linear probability function models were estimated that were analogous to the multinomial logit models presented in the text. As in chapter 3, F-statistics were based on the estimation of equations that included a set of dummy variables for the 400 residential zones used to measure travel time. F values were statistically insignificant at conventional levels, which indicates that the possible presence of error components has not had an important affect on my results. In addition, I again estimated models that allowed for the variance components structure of the disturbance and obtained results very similar to those discussed in the text.

[10] A number of other studies have investigated the relationship between the unemployment rate and the rate of school enrollment (Duncan 1965; Lerman 1972; Edwards 1976; Hill 1979; Gustman and Steinmeier 1981). Results have been highly mixed both within and across these studies.

APPENDIX TO CHAPTER 4

Results Obtained with the Metropolitan Area Variables

Table 4A.1 Implied Partial Derivatives for Metropolitan Area Variables: White Males, 16–17 Years Old
(Asymptotic t-Statistics)

	$P1$[a]	$P2$	$P3$	$P4$	Employed $(P1+P3)$	Enrolled $(P1+P2)$	χ^2
Population of the SMSA	−0.0003	−0.0001	−0.0001	0.0005	−0.0004	−0.0004	1.29
	(0.80)	(0.26)	(0.27)	(0.92)	(0.33)	(0.60)	
Fraction of population black	0.4230	−0.4890	0.0661	−0.0001	0.4891	−0.0660	12.08***
	(2.9240)	(−3.27)	(1.36)	(−0.00)	(3.34)	(0.81)	
Fraction of labor force women	−2.5517	2.4869	−0.1053	0.1709	−2.6569	−0.0648	25.26***
	(4.87)	(4.59)	(0.55)	(0.77)	(4.77)	(0.22)	
Unemployment rate	−0.0252	0.0318	−0.0076	0.0099	−0.0329	0.0066	40.10***
	(4.62)	(5.59)	(3.64)	(0.41)	(5.89)	(2.063)	
Fraction of jobs operatives	2.1271	−2.0152	0.1423	−0.2555	2.2694	0.1119	27.33***
	(4.96)	(4.52)	(0.90)	(1.35)	(5.20)	(0.45)	
Fraction of jobs clerical	2.0141	−1.2551	−0.0240	−0.7385	1.9901	0.7590	7.55*
	(2.03)	(1.83)	(0.07)	(1.87)	(3.21)	(1.31)	
Fraction of jobs service	2.6218	−3.0837	0.3565	0.1059	2.9783	0.4619	9.71**
	(2.69)	(3.06)	(1.00)	(0.25)	(3.01)	(0.83)	
Fraction of jobs craftsmen	0.5413	−0.3141	−0.0725	−0.1555	0.4688	0.2273	0.61
	(0.68)	(0.38)	(0.26)	(0.45)	(0.58)	(0.51)	
Fraction of jobs sales	5.8400	−5.3266	0.4106	−0.9285	6.2506	0.5134	6.65*
	(2.39)	(2.12)	(0.48)	(0.93)	(2.53)	(0.39)	

[a] $P1$ = Enrolled-Employed, $P2$ = Enrolled-Not Employed, $P3$ = Not Enrolled-Employed, $P4$ = Not Enrolled-Not Employed.

The χ^2 statistics reported in the last column are for a Wald test, which indicates whether the travel-time variable has a statistically significant effect on the enrollment-employment state. *** and ** and * indicate significance at the 1 percent, 5 percent, and 10 percent levels, respectively.

Table 4A.2   Implied Partial Derivatives for Metropolitan Area Variables: White Males, 18–19 Years Old
(Asymptotic t-Statistics)

	$P1$[a]	$P2$	$P3$	$P4$	Employed $(P1+P3)$	Enrolled $(P1+P2)$	χ^2
Population of the SMSA	−0.0000	−0.0014	−0.0002	0.0013	−0.0002	−0.0015	1.79
	(0.05)	(3.34)	(0.81)	(1.14)	(0.26)	(1.69)	
Fraction of population black	0.3386	−0.2814	0.1163	−0.1738	0.4549	−0.0572	10.35***
	(2.27)	(1.89)	(0.91)	(−1.60)	(3.15)	(0.32)	
Fraction of labor force women	−1.1398	2.0090	−0.2170	0.6532	−1.3568	−0.8692	14.88***
	(−2.0)	(3.60)	(−0.44)	(−1.61)	(2.47)	(1.31)	
Unemployment rate	−0.0219	0.0162	0.0075	0.0049	−0.0211	−0.0056	19.60***
	(3.94)	(2.95)	(0.15)	(1.22)	(3.90)	(0.86)	
Fraction of jobs operatives	1.0888	−1.5724	−0.3474	−0.8323	0.7414	−0.4837	16.72***
	(2.14)	(3.11)	(−0.78)	(2.28)	(1.49)	(0.81)	
Fraction of jobs clerical	0.3856	−0.8690	−0.2796	−0.7642	0.1060	−0.4834	1.95
	(0.40)	(−0.91)	(−0.33)	(1.06)	(0.12)	(0.42)	
Fraction of jobs service	1.5693	−1.2968	−1.1914	0.9203	0.3779	0.2725	5.72
	(1.44)	(1.21)	(1.24)	(1.13)	(0.36)	(0.21)	
Fraction of jobs craftsmen	−0.1827	0.9230	−0.2581	−0.4830	−0.4408	−0.5080	1.24
	(0.21)	(1.05)	(−0.34)	(−0.75)	(0.51)	(0.74)	
Fraction of jobs sales	0.8194	−8.0118	3.6209	3.5771	4.4408	−7.1725	8.29**
	(0.276)	(2.77)	(1.42)	(1.72)	(1.55)	(2.11)	

[a] $P1$ = Enrolled-Employed, $P2$ = Enrolled-Not Employed, $P3$ = Not Enrolled-Employed, $P4$ = Not Enrolled-Not Employed.

The χ^2 statistics reported in the last column are for a Wald test, which indicates whether the travel-time variable has a statistically significant effect on the enrollment-employment state. *** and ** and * indicate significance at the 1 percent, 5 percent, and 10 percent levels, respectively.

Table 4A.3   Implied Partial Derivatives for Metropolitan Area Variables: Black Males, 16–17 Years Old
(Asymptotic t-Statistics)

	$P1$[a]	$P2$	$P3$	$P4$	Employed $(P1+P3)$	Enrolled $(P1+P2)$	χ^2
Population of the SMSA	−0.0003	−0.0011	−0.0003	−0.0005	−0.0006	0.0008	1.12
	(1.76)	(1.30)	(0.85)	(0.54)	(1.62)	(0.84)	
Fraction of population black	0.1318	−0.1116	−0.0288	0.0086	0.1030	0.0202	2.51
	(1.36)	(0.91)	(0.82)	(0.11)	(1.01)	(0.23)	
Fraction of labor force women	−0.0016	−0.0294	−0.2011	−0.1708	0.1995	−0.0310	1.98
	(0.04)	(0.06)	(1.31)	(0.52)	(0.48)	(0.08)	
Unemployment rate	−0.0102	0.0092	−0.0008	0.0018	−0.0110	−0.0010	6.65*
	(2.49)	(1.80)	(0.50)	(0.55)	(2.54)	(0.27)	
Fraction of jobs operatives	−0.4096	−0.1768	−0.1914	0.4260	−0.6010	−0.2328	5.54
	(1.16)	(0.40)	(1.49)	(1.50)	(1.62)	(0.75)	
Fraction of jobs clerical	0.0561	−0.2501	−0.1336	0.3292	−0.0776	−0.1940	0.42
	(0.07)	(0.25)	(0.42)	(0.49)	(0.10)	(0.26)	
Fraction of jobs service	0.6145	−0.5151	−0.0068	−0.1066	0.6213	0.0994	0.50
	(0.70)	(0.47)	(0.02)	(0.15)	(0.70)	(0.13)	
Fraction of jobs craftsmen	0.8236	0.0880	−0.02111	−0.9366	0.8447	0.9116	3.35
	(1.21)	(6.16)	(0.09)	(1.61)	(1.17)	(1.36)	
Fraction of jobs sales	−0.5710	−1.3901	−0.2600	2.2303	−0.8309	−1.9611	1.93
	(0.28)	(0.54)	(0.37)	(1.34)	(0.38)	(1.09)	

[a] $P1$ = Enrolled-Employed, $P2$ = Enrolled-Not Employed, $P3$ = Not Enrolled-Employed, $P4$ = Not Enrolled-Not Employed.

The χ^2 statistics reported in the last column are for a Wald test, which indicates whether the travel-time variable has a statistically significant effect on the enrollment-employment state. *** and ** and * indicate significance at the 1 percent, 5 percent, and 10 percent levels, respectively.

Table 4A.4 Implied Partial Derivatives for Metropolitan Area Variables: Black Males, 18–19 Years Old
(Asymptotic t-Statistics)

	$P1$[a]	$P2$	$P3$	$P4$	Employed $(P1+P3)$	Enrolled $(P1+P2)$	χ^2
Population of the SMSA	0.0001	0.0001	0.0019	−0.0021	0.0020	0.0001	4.09
	(0.09)	(0.05)	(1.38)	(1.58)	(1.05)	(0.12)	
Fraction of population black	0.2370	0.4606	−0.0434	−0.6542	0.1936	0.6981	24.54***
	(2.41)	(3.07)	(0.45)	(4.76)	(1.55)	(4.46)	
Fraction of labor force women	−0.3454	−0.7840	0.3296	0.1090	0.6749	−0.4391	2.32
	(0.87)	(1.33)	(0.83)	(0.20)	(1.32)	(0.71)	
Unemployment rate	−0.0135	0.0074	−0.0151	0.0213	−0.0287	−0.0062	31.30***
	(3.14)	(1.18)	(3.49)	(3.76)	(5.24)	(0.95)	
Fraction of jobs operatives	−0.8257	0.1078	−0.0661	0.7840	−0.8918	−0.7182	5.86
	(2.20)	(0.19)	(−0.18)	(1.55)	(1.88)	(1.25)	
Fraction of jobs clerical	−0.2618	1.3974	−0.6406	−0.4950	−0.9024	1.1360	1.36
	(0.32)	(1.11)	(0.73)	(0.42)	(0.83)	(0.86)	
Fraction of jobs service	1.7720	1.5607	−0.6740	−2.6587	1.0979	3.3333	6.85*
	(1.92)	(1.14)	(0.73)	(2.13)	(0.94)	(2.32)	
Fraction of jobs craftsmen	1.5463	1.6566	−0.0490	−3.1540	1.4974	3.203	11.69***
	(2.25)	(1.55)	(0.07)	(3.12)	(1.66)	(2.83)	
Fraction of jobs sales	−4.9683	−7.7265	2.6355	10.0593	−2.3328	−12.6951	15.73***
	(2.31)	(2.40)	(1.23)	(3.44)	(0.85)	(3.78)	

[a] $P1$ = Enrolled-Employed, $P2$ = Enrolled-Not Employed, $P3$ = Not Enrolled-Employed, $P4$ = Not Enrolled-Not Employed.

The χ^2 statistics reported in the last column are for a Wald test, which indicates whether the travel-time variable has a statistically significant effect on the enrollment-employment state. *** and ** and * indicate significance at the 1 percent, 5 percent, and 10 percent levels, respectively.

Table 4A.5   Implied Partial Derivatives for Metropolitan Area Variables: Hispanic Males, 16–17 Years Old
(Asymptotic t-Statistics)

	$P1$[a]	$P2$	$P3$	$P4$	Employed $(P1+P3)$	Enrolled $(P1+P2)$	χ^2
Population of the SMSA	0.0008	0.0005	−0.0013	0.0000	−0.0005	0.0013	2.26
	(1.83)	(0.37)	(1.24)	(0.01)	(0.63)	(0.73)	
Fraction of population black	0.3364	−0.1273	−0.1012	−0.1080	0.2351	0.2091	6.59*
	(2.41)	(0.69)	(1.10)	(0.80)	(1.50)	(1.30)	
Fraction of labor force women	−0.5797	0.2772	−0.2906	0.5942	−0.8702	−0.3025	3.36
	(1.09)	(0.42)	(0.86)	(1.32)	(1.47)	(0.54)	
Unemployment rate	−0.0241	0.0368	−0.0093	−0.0034	−0.0334	0.0127	32.48***
	(4.27)	(5.32)	(2.63)	(0.74)	(5.37)	(2.20)	
Fraction of jobs operatives	0.7861	−1.0910	0.3728	−0.0684	1.1590	−0.3047	4.94
	(1.64)	(1.81)	(1.27)	(0.17)	(2.18)	(0.61)	
Fraction of jobs clerical	−0.6956	−0.4867	0.3319	0.8521	−0.3636	−1.1823	1.92
	(0.77)	(0.44)	(0.63)	(1.15)	(0.37)	(1.30)	
Fraction of jobs service	−1.4637	1.4902	−0.3373	0.3115	−1.8011	0.0265	2.05
	(1.26)	(1.04)	(0.52)	(0.33)	(1.43)	(0.03)	
Fraction of jobs craftsmen	−1.4374	−0.3908	0.3667	1.4645	−1.0707	−1.8283	7.57*
	(1.87)	(0.41)	(0.84)	(2.22)	(1.27)	(2.32)	
Fraction of jobs sales	9.4830	−7.7743	1.2694	−2.9841	10.7524	1.7087	17.14***
	(3.82)	(2.61)	(0.90)	(1.55)	(4.00)	(0.72)	

[a] $P1$ = Enrolled-Employed, $P2$ = Enrolled-Not Employed, $P3$ = Not Enrolled-Employed, $P4$ = Not Enrolled-Not Employed.

The χ^2 statistics reported in the last column are for a Wald test, which indicates whether the travel-time variable has a statistically significant effect on the enrollment-employment state. *** and ** and * indicate significance at the 1 percent, 5 percent, and 10 percent levels, respectively.

Table 4A.6　Implied Partial Derivatives for Metropolitan Area Variables: Hispanic Males, 18–19 Years Old
(Asymptotic t-Statistics)

	$P1$[a]	$P2$	$P3$	$P4$	Employed $(P1+P3)$	Enrolled $(P1+P2)$	χ^2
Population of the SMSA	0.0003	−0.0023	−0.0036	0.0056	−0.0033	−0.0020	6.66*
	(0.19)	(1.11)	(1.44)	(2.41)	(1.53)	(0.63)	
Fraction of population black	0.4119	0.2333	−0.5156	−0.1298	−0.1037	0.6452	6.27*
	(2.12)	(0.80)	(1.86)	(0.45)	(0.36)	(1.91)	
Fraction of labor force women	−0.8283	1.8129	0.3630	−1.3499	−0.4652	0.9847	5.35
	(1.13)	(1.76)	(0.37)	(1.41)	(0.45)	(0.82)	
Unemployment rate	−0.0105	0.0226	−0.0215	0.0093	−0.0320	0.0122	9.23**
	(1.35)	(2.18)	(2.07)	(0.97)	(2.98)	(1.00)	
Fraction of jobs operatives	1.2193	−1.3722	−0.9556	1.1103	0.2637	−0.1529	7.11*
	(1.82)	(1.47)	(1.06)	(1.29)	(0.28)	(0.14)	
Fraction of jobs clerical	1.2113	0.7368	0.8083	−2.7609	2.0196	1.9481	3.61
	(0.98)	(0.43)	(0.52)	(1.82)	(1.22)	(0.99)	
Fraction of jobs service	−0.2275	2.1486	−3.0574	1.1381	−3.2848	1.9211	2.81
	(0.14)	(0.95)	(1.53)	(0.59)	(1.52)	(0.75)	
Fraction of jobs craftsmen	0.2665	1.1279	−0.2801	−1.1161	−0.0136	1.3943	0.87
	(0.25)	(0.74)	(0.21)	(0.85)	(0.01)	(0.82)	
Fraction of jobs sales	4.4170	−7.5844	2.8061	0.3619	7.2230	−3.1674	4.26
	(1.33)	(1.73)	(0.71)	(0.09)	(1.69)	(0.63)	

[a] $P1$ = Enrolled-Employed, $P2$ = Enrolled-Not Employed, $P3$ = Not Enrolled-Employed, $P4$ = Not Enrolled-Not Employed.

The χ^2 statistics reported in the last column are for a Wald test, which indicates whether the travel-time variable has a statistically significant effect on the enrollment-employment state. *** and ** and * indicate significance at the 1 percent, 5 percent, and 10 percent levels, respectively.

Table 4A.7　Implied Partial Derivatives for Metropolitan Area Variables: White Females, 16–17 Years Old
(Asymptotic t-Statistics)

	$P1$[a]	$P2$	$P3$	$P4$	Employed $(P1+P3)$	Enrolled $(P1+P2)$	χ^2
Population of the SMSA	−0.0025	0.0031	−0.0000	−0.0006	−0.0025	0.0006	5.61
	(1.10)	(1.49)	(0.08)	(1.14)	(1.14)	(1.01)	
Fraction of population black	0.5014	−0.5059	0.0161	−0.0117	0.5175	−0.0045	13.29***
	(3.53)	(3.48)	(0.40)	(0.20)	(3.61)	(0.06)	
Fraction of labor force women	−1.7965	1.5671	−0.0134	0.2448	−1.8099	−0.2295	11.82***
	(3.37)	(2.88)	(0.10)	(1.10)	(3.38)	(0.88)	
Unemployment rate	−0.0281	0.0295	−0.0009	−0.0006	−0.0290	0.0014	29.03***
	(5.13)	(5.26)	(0.64)	(0.23)	(5.25)	(0.52)	
Fraction of jobs operatives	1.0002	−0.8379	−0.0626	−0.1005	0.9376	0.1623	5.57
	(2.34)	(1.91)	(−0.54)	(0.54)	(2.17)	(0.73)	
Fraction of jobs clerical	0.7766	−1.6235	0.4571	0.3930	1.2337	−0.8470	5.95
	(0.89)	(−1.82)	(1.82)	(1.02)	(1.41)	(1.83)	
Fraction of jobs service	3.7761	−4.3643	0.4863	0.1027	4.2624	−0.5882	21.02***
	(3.91)	(−4.40)	(1.73)	(0.24)	(4.37)	(1.14)	
Fraction of jobs craftsmen	0.3846	−1.3403	0.5725	0.3863	0.9571	−0.9557	8.89**
	(0.48)	(1.62)	(2.64)	(1.12)	(1.18)	(2.31)	
Fraction of jobs sales	−3.1442	2.3827	−0.0682	0.8364	−3.2124	−0.7616	2.23
	(1.33)	(0.98)	(0.12)	(0.86)	(1.35)	(0.67)	

[a] $P1$ = Enrolled-Employed, $P2$ = Enrolled-Not Employed, $P3$ = Not Enrolled-Employed, $P4$ = Not Enrolled-Not Employed.

The χ^2 statistics reported in the last column are for a Wald test, which indicates whether the travel-time variable has a statistically significant effect on the enrollment-employment state. *** and ** and * indicate significance at the 1 percent, 5 percent, and 10 percent levels, respectively.

Table 4A.8 Implied Partial Derivatives for Metropolitan Area Variables: White Females, 18–19 Years Old
(Asymptotic t-Statistics)

	$P1$[a]	$P2$	$P3$	$P4$	Employed $(P1+P3)$	Enrolled $(P1+P2)$	χ^2
Population of the SMSA	−0.0042	0.0013	0.0019	0.0011	−0.0023	−0.0030	9.17**
	(7.62)	(2.65)	(11.42)	(0.88)	(3.21)	(2.87)	
Fraction of population black	0.4801	−0.0279	−0.2399	−0.2124	0.2401	0.4521	10.78**
	(3.03)	(0.19)	(2.34)	(1.74)	(1.61)	(2.70)	
Fraction of labor force women	−0.6789	1.3967	−0.1032	−0.6151	−0.7821	0.7179	7.78**
	(1.18)	(2.69)	(0.28)	(1.37)	(1.45)	(1.18)	
Unemployment rate	−0.0129	0.0089	−0.0073	0.0114	−0.0203	−0.0040	16.07***
	(2.26)	(1.68)	(1.90)	(2.53)	(3.72)	(0.66)	
Fraction of jobs operatives	0.3380	−0.5056	0.1512	0.0164	0.4892	−0.1676	1.41
	(0.68)	(1.11)	(0.46)	(0.04)	(1.03)	(0.32)	
Fraction of jobs clerical	2.3001	−1.7548	−0.8018	0.2567	1.4983	0.5453	8.24**
	(2.35)	(1.94)	(1.23)	(0.33)	(1.61)	(0.52)	
Fraction of jobs service	2.0665	−0.1619	−0.9184	−0.9869	1.1481	1.9046	4.13
	(1.90)	(0.16)	(1.32)	(1.15)	(1.11)	(1.67)	
Fraction of jobs craftsmen	0.4774	0.5088	−0.7574	−0.2291	−0.2799	0.9862	1.96
	(0.56)	(0.66)	(1.38)	(0.33)	(0.35)	(1.08)	
Fraction of jobs sales	0.1024	−6.6745	2.5566	4.0184	2.6590	−6.5721	8.05**
	(0.04)	(2.64)	(1.41)	(1.81)	(1.01)	(2.20)	

[a] $P1$ = Enrolled-Employed, $P2$ = Enrolled-Not Employed, $P3$ = Not Enrolled-Employed, $P4$ = Not Enrolled-Not Employed.

The χ^2 statistics reported in the last column are for a Wald test, which indicates whether the travel-time variable has a statistically significant effect on the enrollment-employment state. *** and ** and * indicate significance at the 1 percent, 5 percent, and 10 percent levels, respectively.

Table 4A.9   Implied Partial Derivatives for Metropolitan Area Variables: Black Females, 16–17 Years Old
(Asymptotic *t*-Statistics)

	$P1$[a]	$P2$	$P3$	$P4$	Employed $(P1+P3)$	Enrolled $(P1+P2)$	χ^2
Population of the SMSA	−0.0012	0.0008	0.0001	0.0004	−0.0012	−0.0001	1.32
	(1.04)	(0.60)	(0.25)	(0.37)	(0.97)	(0.43)	
Fraction of population black	0.1808	−0.1932	0.0014	0.0113	0.1821	−0.0122	3.83
	(1.92)	(1.63)	(0.06)	(0.14)	(1.89)	(0.15)	
Fraction of labor force women	−0.7882	0.8113	−0.0680	0.0455	−0.8563	0.0231	4.68
	(2.03)	(1.68)	(0.68)	(0.135)	(2.15)	(0.07)	
Unemployment rate	−0.0103	0.0068	−0.0011	0.0046	−0.0113	−0.0035	7.57**
	(2.34)	(1.28)	(0.98)	(1.28)	(2.54)	(0.94)	
Fraction of jobs operatives	−0.0446	−0.0975	0.0939	0.0488	0.0493	−0.1421	1.34
	(0.12)	(0.22)	(1.15)	(0.17)	(0.14)	(0.95)	
Fraction of jobs clerical	0.5703	0.3880	−0.3792	−0.5871	0.1911	0.9583	3.86
	(0.72)	(0.39)	(1.68)	(0.85)	(0.23)	(1.34)	
Fraction of jobs service	1.0748	−0.1370	0.0119	−0.9627	1.0867	0.9378	2.70
	(1.19)	(0.12)	(0.05)	(1.28)	(1.18)	(1.21)	
Fraction of jobs craftsmen	1.0084	0.2429	−0.2558	−1.0093	0.7527	1.2514	5.97
	(1.43)	(0.27)	(1.41)	(1.61)	(1.04)	(1.94)	
Fraction of jobs sales	−0.5733	−0.8843	0.2646	1.2094	−0.3087	−1.4576	0.79
	(0.28)	(0.35)	(0.52)	(0.71)	(0.14)	(0.83)	

[a] $P1$ = Enrolled-Employed, $P2$ = Enrolled-Not Employed, $P3$ = Not Enrolled-Employed, $P4$ = Not Enrolled-Not Employed.

The χ^2 statistics reported in the last column are for a Wald test, which indicates whether the travel-time variable has a statistically significant effect on the enrollment-employment state. *** and ** and * indicate significance at the 1 percent, 5 percent, and 10 percent levels, respectively.

Table 4A.10   Implied Partial Derivatives for Metropolitan Area Variables: Black Females, 18–19 Years Old
(Asymptotic *t*-Statistics)

	$P1$[a]	$P2$	$P3$	$P4$	Employed $(P1+P3)$	Enrolled $(P1+P2)$	χ^2
Population of the SMSA	−0.0019	0.0026	0.0013	−0.0021	−0.0006	0.0007	6.20*
	(1.36)	(1.33)	(1.29)	(1.06)	(0.40)	(0.29)	
Fraction of population black	0.1613	−0.0436	−0.1357	0.0231	0.0256	0.1130	4.34
	(1.36)	(0.27)	(1.68)	(0.13)	(0.19)	(0.60)	
Fraction of labor force women	0.5897	−0.1054	−0.5968	0.1126	−0.0070	0.4841	4.42
	(1.25)	(0.15)	(1.80)	(0.17)	(0.01)	(0.66)	
Unemployment rate	−0.0119	0.0021	−0.0073	0.0170	−0.0191	−0.0098	13.17***
	(2.30)	(0.28)	(2.10)	(2.38)	(3.31)	(1.30)	
Fraction of jobs operatives	−1.0924	−0.3004	0.6110	0.7825	−0.4814	−1.3931	9.08*
	(2.40)	(0.45)	(2.05)	(1.21)	(0.95)	(2.00)	
Fraction of jobs clerical	−0.0167	−2.5831	0.5523	2.0497	0.5355	−2.6000	3.11
	(0.02)	(1.70)	(0.80)	(1.37)	(0.47)	(1.62)	
Fraction of jobs service	1.5632	2.5431	−1.5134	−2.5956	0.0498	4.1063	7.85**
	(1.45)	(1.60)	(2.07)	(1.69)	(0.04)	(2.50)	
Fraction of jobs craftsmen	2.5117	−0.5117	−0.7472	−1.2540	1.7644	2.0060	10.26**
	(3.08)	(0.40)	(1.29)	(0.99)	(1.89)	(1.48)	
Fraction of jobs sales	−7.0257	−4.9722	6.1464	5.8574	−0.8793	−11.9981	17.93***
	(2.68)	(1.29)	(3.46)	(1.58)	(0.30)	(2.98)	

[a] $P1$ = Enrolled-Employed, $P2$ = Enrolled-Not Employed, $P3$ = Not Enrolled-Employed, $P4$ = Not Enrolled-Not Employed.

The χ^2 statistics reported in the last column are for a Wald test, which indicates whether the travel-time variable has a statistically significant effect on the enrollment-employment state. *** and ** and * indicate significance at the 1 percent, 5 percent, and 10 percent levels, respectively.

Table 4A.11　Implied Partial Derivatives for Metropolitan Area Variables: Hispanic Females, 16–17 Years Old
(Asymptotic t-Statistics)

	$P1$[a]	$P2$	$P3$	$P4$	Employed $(P1+P3)$	Enrolled $(P1+P2)$	χ^2
Population of the SMSA	−0.0023	0.0023	−0.0003	0.0004	−0.0027	−0.0000	2.99
	(1.48)	(1.37)	(0.54)	(0.29)	(1.67)	(0.02)	
Fraction of population black	0.2961	0.2254	−0.1430	−0.3789	0.1531	0.5216	10.93**
	(2.13)	(1.18)	(1.64)	(2.47)	(0.99)	(2.99)	
Fraction of labor force women	−0.1326	0.1754	−0.3552	0.3128	−0.4879	0.0427	2.04
	(0.25)	(0.26)	(1.26)	(0.63)	(0.86)	(0.07)	
Unemployment rate	−0.0126	0.0212	−0.0117	0.0031	−0.0243	0.0086	22.79***
	(2.33)	(3.12)	(3.88)	(0.65)	(4.12)	(1.55)	
Fraction of jobs operatives	0.3402	0.0301	0.2634	−0.6343	0.6036	0.3702	3.42
	(0.73)	(0.05)	(1.06)	(1.42)	(1.20)	(0.73)	
Fraction of jobs clerical	0.5603	−0.8320	0.1233	0.1486	0.6836	−0.2717	0.66
	(0.65)	(0.77)	(0.28)	(0.19)	(0.74)	(0.31)	
Fraction of jobs service	−0.1306	−1.4956	0.9562	0.6706	0.8256	−1.6262	3.93
	(0.12)	(1.06)	(1.85)	(0.67)	(0.69)	(1.44)	
Fraction of jobs craftsmen	0.2928	−2.1143	0.0477	1.7756	0.3405	−1.8216	7.53**
	(0.39)	(−2.20)	(0.14)	(2.58)	(0.42)	(2.36)	
Fraction of jobs sales	1.5081	1.8747	0.8883	−3.4746	1.5964	3.3828	2.78
	(0.63)	(0.63)	(0.08)	(1.63)	(0.63)	(1.41)	

[a] $P1$ = Enrolled-Employed, $P2$ = Enrolled-Not Employed, $P3$ = Not Enrolled-Employed, $P4$ = Not Enrolled-Not Employed.

The χ^2 statistics reported in the last column are for a Wald test, which indicates whether the travel-time variable has a statistically significant effect on the enrollment-employment state. *** and ** and * indicate significance at the 1 percent, 5 percent, and 10 percent levels, respectively.

Table 4A.12   Implied Partial Derivatives for Metropolitan Area Variables: Hispanic Females, 18–19 Years Old
(Asymptotic t-Statistics)

	$P1$[a]	$P2$	$P3$	$P4$	Employed $(P1+P3)$	Enrolled $(P1+P2)$	χ^2
Population of the SMSA	−0.0003	−0.0037	0.0012	0.0028	0.0010	−0.0040	1.45
	(0.11)	(1.20)	(0.60)	(0.90)	(0.32)	(1.24)	
Fraction of population black	0.3018	0.50	−0.2513	−0.5563	0.0506	0.8065	4.37
	(1.34)	(1.52)	(0.99)	(1.56)	(0.17)	(2.07)	
Fraction of labor force women	0.0252	4.1026	−1.4175	−2.7155	−1.3923	4.1278	11.67***
	(0.03)	(3.35)	(1.64)	(2.20)	(1.27)	(3.00)	
Unemployment rate	−0.0213	0.0418	−0.0114	−0.0092	−0.0327	0.0205	13.60***
	(2.21)	(3.27)	(1.23)	(0.71)	(2.78)	(1.42)	
Fraction of jobs operatives	0.1094	−3.5822	0.6599	2.8182	0.7692	−3.4728	10.37**
	(0.13)	(3.13)	(0.85)	(2.50)	(0.76)	(2.71)	
Fraction of jobs clerical	0.8960	1.3448	−1.1989	−1.0438	−0.3029	2.2407	1.17
	(0.6024)	(0.65)	(0.85)	(0.53)	(0.17)	(0.98)	
Fraction of jobs service	−2.3554	−1.5085	2.2226	1.6444	−0.1328	−3.8639	2.81
	(1.23)	(0.58)	(1.28)	(0.67)	(0.06)	(1.36)	
Fraction of jobs craftsmen	−1.0325	2.2701	0.3110	−1.5515	0.7215	1.2375	2.41
	(0.81)	(1.27)	(0.28)	(0.94)	(0.48)	(0.64)	
Fraction of jobs sales	10.8392	−5.6267	−4.7213	−0.4921	6.1179	5.2125	8.24**
	(2.64)	(1.08)	(1.36)	(0.10)	(1.30)	(0.91)	

[a] $P1$ = Enrolled-Employed, $P2$ = Enrolled-Not Employed, $P3$ = Not Enrolled-Employed, $P4$ = Not Enrolled-Not Employed.

The χ^2 statistics reported in the last column are for a Wald test, which indicates whether the travel-time variable has a statistically significant effect on the enrollment-employment state. *** and ** and * indicate significance at the 1 percent, 5 percent, and 10 percent levels, respectively.

5

Policy Conclusions

This study has provided a considerable amount of evidence on how intraurban job accessibility, as well as other factors, impinge upon the employment and school enrollment decisions of teenagers. An assessment of the policy relevance of the evidence yields a number of important findings. In this chapter these findings are thoroughly discussed, along with related work in the literature. The principal conclusion of this discussion is that attempts should be made to improve the intraurban job accessibility of central city minority youth.

The results of this study strongly suggest that intraurban job accessibility, defined in terms of the distance to available jobs, has an important effect on the job probabilities of most teenage youths. Generally, the effect is present regardless of the teenager's age, family income level, gender, race, enrollment status, or location within the metropolitan area (i.e., central city versus suburban ring). The only stratification of the sample that does not yield robust job access effects is based on the size of the metropolitan area. Job access is found to have little or no effect on the job probabilities of teenagers, especially those who are out of school, living in small metropolitan areas. Except for the latter group, the results imply that policies to improve job accessibility will increase youth employment. Policies to improve the intraurban job accessibility of youths in general, however, are probably not warranted, since the employment rates of white teenagers are not perceived to be a problem by most observers.

As I documented in chapter 1, the employment rates of white male teenagers have been remarkably stable over the entire postwar period, while the secular trend in the employment rates of white female teenagers has been continuously upward. As noted by Freeman and Wise (1982), "constant references to *the* youth employment problem, as if all or the majority of young persons has difficulty obtaining jobs, appear to misinterpret the nature of the difficulty." The true nature of the difficulty is that minority youth employment rates, especially within the central cities of large metropolitan areas, are unacceptably high relative to the employment rates of white youths. It is, therefore, of considerable interest that the magnitude of the estimated effect of job access on job probability is particularly large in the case of black and Hispanic youths living within large central cities and that these youths have the worst job access of any of the groups included in my analysis. My estimates suggest that a five-minute reduction in expected commuting time by automobile, which is roughly equal to a one standard deviation change, would increase the employment rates of central city black and Hispanic teenagers who are not in school by 26 percent and 17 percent, respectively. The percentage increases for youth who are in school are even higher, namely 36 percent and 48 percent, respectively. Policies to improve the job accessibility of central city minority youths are clearly recommended by these results.

The results obtained for minority central city youths are striking on two accounts. First, they are completely at odds with evidence provided by the three previous studies (Osterman 1980; Ellwood 1986; Leonard 1986b) that have focused on job access as an explanation for the black youth employment problem. Since these studies have all found that the job access effect is trivial in magnitude, the tendency might be to accept the majority position rather than the one advanced by this study. I believe this would be a mistake for a number of reasons. First, the methodological shortcomings of previous studies are very apparent. The most obvious problem has been the simultaneity that exists between employment status and residential location, which tends to bias the estimates of prior studies toward zero. This problem is circumvented in the present study by restricting the analysis to a group whose residential locations can legitimately be considered as exogenous, namely teenagers who are still living at home.

There is, of course, a cost associated with this restriction; namely, that my results cannot be generalized to the group of teenagers who are no longer living at home. Since this group is small, the benefits of my approach to the simultaneity problem clearly outweigh the costs. Second, the fact that my results are robust across different samples, different estimating techniques and specifications, and different groups strongly suggests that the observed job access effects are genuine and not just statistical artifacts. Finally, as emphasized in chapter 2, it should not be surprising that my results support the spatial mismatch hypothesis as it applies to youths, since that portion of the general mismatch literature that has provided reliable evidence has consistently found that access is important. If greater distances to jobs impinge on the economic welfare of black adults, we would certainly expect that youths would also be affected, since they are more dependent than adults on nearby jobs.

The other striking feature of the results obtained for central city minorities are the magnitudes of the effects that job access is found to have on the probability that the youth has a job. While these magnitudes are large, they are not implausibly so. For example, consider the group that policymakers are most concerned about, namely nonenrolled black teenagers. My results indicate that a five-minute reduction in their expected commuting time would increase their job probability by .075. Holding other factors constant, this would cause the mean employment rate of this group to rise from .294 to .369, which represents a 26 percent increase. For this group, a five-minute reduction in travel time is approximately a 20 percent decline in their expected commute; hence, the hypothesized improvement in job access should be considered substantial.

It is also important to remember that travel time is measured for only those workers who drive to work. Since many low-wage central city workers are expected to be reverse commuters, the assumption that a considerable portion of the typical trip involves high-speed travel along a radial expressway is not unreasonable. Also, by traveling against traffic, average travel speeds are higher because congestion is less problem; therefore, a five-minute reduction in travel time most probably means that the average job is moving from three to five miles closer to a youth's residence. Since central city minority youths overwhelmingly rely on transportation modes other than automobiles for their journey to work, these distances could easily have an important influence on a youth's information regarding available jobs and his/her cost of travel.[1]

Another issue raised by my results concerns the residential mobility of central city minorities: if better access to jobs has an important effect on their economic welfare, why don't they move their homes closer to where jobs are located? For blacks, numerous studies have shown that their residential locations are constrained by discrimination in the housing market. While much less research has been done for Hispanics, the evidence that does exist suggests that they too encounter significant discrimination in the housing market (Greene 1981; Hakken 1979; Franklin et al. 1983, Turner et al. 1991a).[2] In addition, the ability of blacks and Hispanics to relocate in response to job decentralization is constrained by their relatively low income levels. Generally, housing becomes less affordable farther from the city center, since at greater distances houses are newer, larger, and located in nicer neighborhoods.

While the results of this study indicate that job access is important to our understanding of the relatively low employment rates of black and Hispanic youths, they also make it clear that other causal factors are obviously at work. The decompositions presented in our Philadelphia study, combined with those presented in chapters 3 and 4, indicate that from one-fifth to one-half of the racial difference in employment rates can be attributed to differences in job access, depending on the youth group considered. This leaves considerable room for alternative hypotheses to also play a role in our understanding of the black and Hispanic youth employment problems. In the case of black youths, two alternative hypotheses are frequently mentioned: (1) employers discriminate against blacks in making their hiring decisions; and (2) negative concentration effects exist within central city ghettos.

As discussed in chapter 3, "concentration effects" are the label that Wilson has attached to the influence of ghetto neighborhood characteristics on individual behavior. According to Wilson, the outmigration from the ghetto of upwardly mobile blacks and the loss of the social organizations once supported by these blacks—such as churches—has reduced the number of positive role models for low-income people. This in turn has resulted in an increase in deviant behavior within the ghetto, which partially manifests itself in young blacks having a lower willingness to work in the mainstream economy. The evidence of this study is consistent with the discrimination hypothesis, but contrary to the concentration effects hypothesis.

The results consistent with the discrimination hypothesis are those obtained with two of the metropolitan area descriptors: the percentage of the metropolitan population who are black, and the percentage of the metropolitan labor force who are adult females with no more than a high school education. Increases in percent black are found to increase the job probabilities of white teenagers. This result is consistent with the hypothesis that whites encounter less competition for available jobs if they are competing against blacks rather than other whites, because employers are racially prejudiced. Increases in the percentage of the labor force who are less-educated adult women are found to have a negative effect on the job probabilities of whites, but they have no effect on the job probabilities of blacks. These results suggest that employers view adult women and white youths as substitutes, but they do not consider adult women and black youths as substitutes. Once again, this is suggestive of employer discrimination. The evidence provided in support of the discrimination hypothesis implies that the hiring practices of employers should be monitored more closely. Strict guidelines that attempt to provide blacks fair treatment in promotion and firing decisions are already in place. Such guidelines should be extended to the hiring decision.

Regarding concentration effects, central city black youths are not found to have a lower probability of having a job in comparison to black youths living in suburban areas. In fact, after controlling for individual and family characteristics and intraurban job access, the results suggest that just the opposite is true. If concentration effects are an important source of black youth joblessness, we would certainly expect that the residual effect of a central city residential location on the probability of having a job would be negative rather than positive in sign. Of course, these results in no way preclude the possibility that concentration effects make a contribution to the many other social problems that tend to plague central city ghettos.[3]

A possible concern with policies designed to improve the intraurban job accessibility of central city teenagers is that they may cause school enrollment to decline. Duncan (1965) first expressed this concern over 25 years ago: "These results suggest, however, that a successful policy to reduce unemployment among dropouts might well have the side effect of encouraging boys to drop out of school before high-school graduation" (p. 134). The findings of this study suggest that Duncan's concern is unwarranted in the case of job access improvement policies. Better access to jobs is found to have a neutral effect on the school enrollment decision of younger teenagers, except in the case of black males from families with low income. For these youths, a small, but statistically significant, increase in school enrollment is observed. For most groups of older teenagers, an improvement in job access is also found to increase school enrollment. This result is obtained for white males, white females, black males, and Hispanic females. The intuition behind these positive school enrollment effects is that having part-time job opportunities located nearby enables youths to satisfy their desire for current earnings without dropping out of high school.

A positive school enrollment effect from better job access is not found for older black female and older Hispanic male teenagers. The failure to observe a positive school enrollment effect for black females is not surprising, since a high percentage of this group who are out of school are mothers of young children. This implies that they are less likely than other teenagers to be on the margin between the not enrolled-not employed state and the enrolled-employed state. The policy implication is that job access improvement policies need to be combined with subsidized child care and/or policies to reduce unwed pregnancies. Such policies would help enable black females to respond to better job access in the same manner as the other groups: the probability of the enrolled-employed state would rise and there would be a corresponding decline in the probability of the not enrolled-not employed state. In the case of older Hispanic males, there is no reason to expect that their behavior should differ from that of the other groups for which better job access has resulted in higher school enrollment. The absence of a positive school enrollment effect for them, therefore, may reflect the greater difficulties encountered in reliably estimating job access effects for Hispanic youths.

The magnitude of the job access effect on school enrollment is largest for older black male teenagers. A five-minute reduction in travel time would cause their enrollment rate to increase by about 10 percent, regardless of family income level. Since job access policies would most likely be targeted to this group, the presence of strong positive school enrollment effects adds considerable appeal to these policies. This appeal is further enhanced by my finding that these effects are the result of a decline in the probabilities of the not enrolled-not employed state and an increase in the probability of the enrolled-employed state. Better job access not only has a desirable effect on school enrollment, but also decreases the likelihood that the youth is in the state that is probably most inimical to his own welfare and that of society. For example, evidence provided by Viscusi (1986) for black male youths indicates that those in the not enrolled-not employed state are more likely to have committed a crime in the past month, or year, in comparison to those in the other three enrollment-employment states. There is reason, therefore, to believe that better job access would not only increase employment and enrollment among black youths, but would also decrease their relatively high involvement in criminal activity.

The findings that better job access reduces the probability that the teenager is in the not enrolled-not employed state and increases the probability of school enrollment are not without precedent. Similar findings have been reported by Farkas et al. (1983) in their evaluation of the effects of the Youth Incentive Enrollment Pilot Projects (hereafter referred to as Youth Incentive Projects) which were funded by the Youth Employment and Demonstration Project Act (hereafter referred to as Youth Demonstration Act) of 1977. Youth Incentive Projects offered a minimum wage job, part time during the school year and full time during the summer, as an entitlement to 16 to 19-year-olds from low-income households who had not yet graduated from high school. During the school year participating youths were required to be in school. Summer jobs were available to program eligibles who had been enrolled in school during the preceding spring, but there was no stipulation that the youths had to return to school in the fall. Farkas et al. first calculated the percentage of days during the preprogram period (January 1977 to March 1978) and the program period (March 1978 to August 1980) that each eligible teenager spent in the four enrollment-employment states.

Program effects were then estimated by fitting ordinary least squares regression models for the percentage of time spent in each state during the program period. Equations were estimated for only black youths. The independent variables included a dummy variable indicating residence in a program site, the percentages of time spent in each of the school/work states in the preprogram period, and a number of sociodemographic control variables. The results indicated that Youth Incentive Projects altered the percentage of days spent in each of the states as follows: an increase of 18.6 percentage points in the enrolled-employed state, a decrease of 16.8 percentage points in the enrolled-not employed state, an increase of 3.5 percentage points in the not enrolled-employed state, and a decrease of 5.3 percentage points in the not enrolled-not employed state. As the result of these changes, the percentage of days spent in school went up by 1.8 percentage points. Due to differences in the samples and methodologies employed, it is not possible to meaningfully compare the magnitudes of the effects found by Farkas et al. and those obtained from my multinomial logit analysis. The two sets of results are qualitatively similar, however, which strengthens my argument in favor of the adoption of job access improvement policies for central city minority youth.

In addition to the concern expressed by Duncan, a second possible school-related problem might arise if job access improvement policies are adopted. For many of the teenager groups, better job access is found to reduce the probability of the enrolled-not employed state and increase the probability of the enrolled-employed state. The issue is whether employment during high school impairs the teenager's school performance by distracting him/her from his/her schoolwork. This issue has been investigated by D'Amico (1984) using data from the 1979 through 1982 waves of the National Longitudinal Surveys of the Labor Market Experience of Youth. His results show that, regardless of the sex or race of a youth, more extensive work involvement during the school year does not reduce class rank. In fact, he found that employment has a positive and statistically significant effect on the class standing of white males. The effect for the other race/sex groups is also positive and approaches statistical significance at the 5 percent level. He suggests that these results are congruent with the notion that work fosters personality traits—e.g., perseverance, dependability, and consistency—that are advantageous to students. D'Amico also found that as long as youths work fewer than 20 hours a week there is no deleterious effect of employment on the probability of dropping out of high school. In fact, for most race/sex groups, working at a modest intensity level was found to reduce the likelihood of dropping out.

My results, as well as those of Farkas et al. and D'Amico, suggest that having a part-time job increases the probability of school enrollment. This finding has an obvious bearing on the desirability of proposed changes to the school schedule that would increase the length of the school day or the school year (National Commission on Excellence in Education 1983). Since more time in school means less opportunity to work, such changes may well have a negative school enrollment effect. This possible effect needs to be estimated and carefully considered in evaluating these changes. One way to mitigate this effect, if it is found to be of consequence, would be to better integrate work experience into the high school curriculum. If time spent working counted toward school attendance, increasing the time required to obtain the high school degree might have a less negative effect on school enrollment.

Having stated my case that efforts should be made to improve the intraurban job accessibility of central city minority youth, the question remains how operationally can this best be done? Because many possible policy options exist, this is a complex question, which requires additional research. For example, research is needed to determine the relative importance of the mechanisms by which an absence of nearby jobs actually impinges on youth employment. To review, there are two basic mechanisms. One mechanism is that youths are unable or unwilling to make a longer journey to work, because of the time and/or money costs associated with the trip. The other mechanism is suggested by the work of Holzer (1987). Using a sample of out-of-school youths 16 to 23 years old, he finds that the most frequently used methods of job search for blacks and whites are checking with friends and relatives and making direct applications without referrals. He also finds that these two informal methods account for almost 70 percent of jobs obtained by whites and almost 60 percent of those obtained by blacks.

The heavy reliance on informal methods of search, rather than on formal methods, such as contacting a private or state employment agency, suggests that the farther away jobs are located from a youth's residence, the less likely it is that he/she will know about them. The relative importance of the transportation and information mechanisms as underlying causes for the effect that job access has on youth employment is unknown. Since such knowledge is crucial in the formulation of appropriate policies, this issue deserves careful consideration in future research.

While the results of this study do not resolve the transportation versus information issue, they do suggest that both mechanisms are probably important. Consider the findings obtained from both the job-probability equations of chapter 3 and the multinomial logit equations of chapter 4 that show that there is little relationship between family income and the strength of the job access effect on job probabilities. Since youth from families with higher incomes have greater access to automobile transportation, if transportation were the sole mechanism by which job access affected employment, we would expect the magnitude of the effect to decline as family income rises. The fact that this does not occur suggests that the information mechanism is relevant. Consider also the findings of chapter 3, which show that the job access effect is generally smaller for nonenrolled, in comparison to enrolled, youths. Since both of these groups rely on informal methods of job search, it is unlikely that one group has a decided advantage over the other in their knowledge about more distant jobs. Transportation costs per unit distance, however, are clearly lower for nonenrolled youths. They have a lower opportunity cost of travel time and are able to amortize both the time and monetary costs of commuting over a longer workday. These results, therefore, suggest that the transportation mechanism is also relevant.

As mentioned above, many policy options can be placed under the general heading of "job access improvement policies," and, in turn, classified into three categories: (1) policies to reduce distances between residential locations of minority teenagers and locations of available jobs, (2) policies to improve minority teenagers' knowledge of more distant job openings, and (3) policies to reduce transportation costs of minority teenagers, without changing job or residential locations. The policies in the first category can be broken down into suburban dispersal strategies, ghetto development policies, and job creation programs. These alternatives, which are discussed in the appendix to this chapter, have long been debated among urban economists. Common features include their political complexity and considerable expense. Nevertheless, the benefits realized from implementing one or more of these policies may well justify the significant hurdles that must be overcome. As the appendix makes clear, before we can make this determination, considerably more research is needed on the effects of each of the three policy options.

In comparison to policies that attempt to alter residential or job locations, programs to improve a teenager's knowledge of more distant job opportunities and reduce his/her travel costs to these jobs are more practical from both a fiscal and political perspective. I, therefore, believe we should focus our attention on these alternatives for the simple reason that the problems of central city minority youth addressed in this book deserve an immediate response. In addition, as I identify below, there are reasons to believe that these policies would be effective.

Regarding the provision of job market information, I am aware of no research that has dealt explicitly with the employment effects that would result from providing central city minority youths with better information on available jobs. This is a fertile area for experimentation, since there are a number of strategies that could be adopted at relatively low cost to enhance a youth's knowledge of jobs outside his/her immediate residential area. Examples of such strategies follow.

The Job Training Partnership Act of 1982 funds Private Industry Councils (PICs) at the local level to provide job training and job placement assistance to disadvantaged people, including youths. Central cities and suburban counties each have their own PICs. As Hughes

(1989a) has noted, central city PICs are often people banks, while suburban PICs are job banks. If PICs were established at the regional level, or if local PICs were part of a metropolitan-wide federation, minority youths enrolled in these programs would gain information on jobs throughout the metropolitan area.

A frequently mentioned proposal to ameliorate labor market imbalances in the general economy is the establishment of computerized job-bank systems. Such systems, which would inform job applicants of all listed jobs throughout the area for which they are qualified, could be established for metropolitan area youths. Another approach would be to facilitate the minority youth's search for a suburban job. For example, transportation could be provided to take these teenagers to those areas — e.g., suburban shopping malls — where worker shortages exist, and enable them to apply directly for available positions.

The category of job access improvement policies that holds the greatest promise of alleviating joblessness among central city minority youths is one that would attempt to reduce transportation costs incurred in holding a suburban job. The radial public transit routes characterizing most metropolitan areas are designed to serve incommuters. They do not meet the transportation needs of reverse commuters, because these workers generally have no economical means to travel from the suburban bus depot or train station to the job site. The job is not likely to be close to a suburban transit stop, since radial transit lines diverge to wide spacing in the suburbs, and jobs are not concentrated near them. In addition, reverse commuters frequently work nonstandard hours and quite frequently find that public transit has shut down for the day by the time they leave work.

The leading advocate of restructuring transit systems to better serve reverse commuters is Hughes (1989a). He suggests that such restructuring "might include modifying routes, schedules, and fares within public transit systems, as well as subsidizing private automobile costs (insurance, fuel, etc.)." He also identifies van-pooling as another option. In many metropolitan areas, special transportation from the central city to the suburbs is provided by state and local governments, nonprofit community groups, and consortia of suburban employers. In addition, the Federal Urban Mass Transit Administration has awarded grants to 14 reverse-commuting projects in 12 different metropolitan areas since 1987. Hughes (1989b) has conducted a survey of the 50 largest metropolitan areas and has found that in one-half of these areas there was a specific transportation component to an employment program for the poor and/or low-income workers. Considerable interest, therefore, exists in job access improvement policies that attempt to reduce the transportation costs incurred by reverse commuters; however, none of the reverse commuter programs currently existing around the country has been evaluated to determine its effectiveness. This is unfortunate, since much could be learned by looking at the variety of programs currently under way.

Evaluations of the federally sponsored Mass Transportation Demonstration Projects were conducted in the late 1960s in selected metropolitan areas. These evaluations indicated that the provision of special bus transportation from the central city to suburban work concentrations had little effect on the unemployment rates of central city low-skilled workers (Kalachck and Gocring 1970). It is unlikcly, however, that these same results would be obtained by a study of the more recent reverse-commuter experiments, since the spatial mismatch problem has undoubtedly worsened over the past 30 years.

An important concern from the perspective of this study is whether van-pooling would improve the job accessibility of enrolled central city minority teenagers. Even with the saving in time that should result from the use of vans, the trip to the suburbs may be prohibitedly expensive in terms of a teenager's time in light of school responsibilities. To the extent that teenagers choose to work on weekends, however, the time costs of the trip are less a problem. In addition, the mean travel times for residential zones estimated in this study indicate that youths living in the inner suburbs have the best access to jobs. This suggests that central city youths are more likely to find a job in the inner, rather than the outer, suburbs. In all but the very largest metropolitan areas, a van traveling from the ghetto against traffic can probably reach jobs located within the inner suburban ring in less than one-half an hour.

Van-pooling and other reverse commuting strategies have a number of promising features. First, anecdotal evidence reported in many newspaper and magazine articles suggests that a shortage of low-skill workers in suburban areas exists and that suburban employers are dealing with the shortage by subsidizing the travel costs of reverse commuters (Peirce 1988; Brownstein 1989; Greene and Carton 1986; Foderaro 1990; Roberts 1990; McCosh 1990; Davidson 1989; Beasley 1990). This suggests that there may be sufficient profit for entrepreneurs to step in and provide reverse-commuting services. In addition, the existence of shortages of labor within the suburbs implies that it may be possible to provide reverse commuters with jobs without taking jobs away from suburban residents.

Second, from the broader perspective of social welfare, encouraging reverse commuting may expedite the long-term goal of residential integration. Minorities who reverse commute are bound to learn more about suburban housing alternatives, which may facilitate their moving to the suburbs. Furthermore, there may be multiplier effects to the extent that reverse commuters carry back to the ghetto information on suburban housing and job opportunities that benefit their brethren. Finally, as Hughes (1987) has noted, the integration of suburban workplaces in the short run may foster attitudinal changes that will allow for integrated neighborhoods in the long run.

In conclusion, despite the need for additional research, this study has taken an important step forward in understanding the minority youth employment problem. The results show that minority youths have relatively poor access to jobs, especially in large central cities where joblessness is rampant. Of more importance, the poor job access of these youths is found to have a nontrivial negative effect on both their probability of having a job and their probability of completing a high school education. Since both the low employment rate of minority youths and their high rate of dropping out of school have become problems of crisis proportions, my hope is that this study will motivate greater experiments with job access improvement policies.

NOTES

[1] For example, in 1980 only 13 percent of minority teenagers living in the city of Philadelphia who held jobs commuted to work by private automobile, according to the 1980 Public-Use Sample.

[2] All of these studies are based on fair-housing audits, which involved sending whites and otherwise comparable Hispanics to the same realty office or rental housing complex. The results of Turner and her colleagues are particularly interesting, since they are based on a national fair-housing audit study that measured discrimination against both blacks and Hispanics. They found that the incidence of discrimination, namely, the share of cases in which the minority partner of the audit team received less favorable treatment than his/her majority partner, was 53 percent for black renters, 46 percent for Hispanic renters, 59 percent for black homebuyers, and 56 percent for Hispanic homebuyers. These results suggest that blacks and Hispanics encounter significant and roughly equal discrimination in the housing market.

[3] The empirical literature on concentration effects is critically reviewed in Jencks and Mayer (1990b).

[4] Eight of these grants were made to public-housing tenant management organizations in eight cities (St. Louis, Chicago, Cleveland, New Orleans, Washington, Jersey City, Boston, and Rochester) to inaugurate transportation services that will be owned and operated by the public-housing residents. At the time this book went to press, only three of the organizations had developed a reverse-commuting service. Of these three, only the service provided by the LeClaire Courts Resident Management Association (Chicago) could be considered a success. This service transports 85 people per day from LeClaire Courts, which is located on Chicago's southwest side, to workplaces in suburban Dupage County. The reasons for the inability of most of the tenant management organizations to establish transportation services for their residents have not been identified. The six grants that did not go to tenant management organizations are part of the Urban Mass Transit Administration's Entrepreneurial Services Program. Five of these projects have succeeded in starting-up reverse-commuting services.

APPENDIX TO CHAPTER 5

Suburban Dispersal, Ghetto Development,
and Job Creation Programs

The purpose of this appendix is to describe the various policy options that exist to reduce the distances between the residential locations of minorities and the locations of available jobs. These options include suburban dispersal strategies, ghetto development policies, and job creation programs. Dispersal strategies seek to decentralize the residences of minorities from the central city to those suburban areas where jobs are located. Policies to economically develop central city ghettos attempt to generate private sector job opportunities for less-educated minority workers. Job creation programs would provide subsidized employment for minorities either in the private or public sectors. The arguments that have been made in favor of and against the use of each option are reviewed. I also discuss the limited existing evidence that has a bearing on the probable success of individual policies.

The principal advocates of suburban dispersal of the minority population have been Kain (1985), Downs (1973), and Orfield (1985). The case in favor of dispersal involves more than just improving the job accessibility of minorities, since it would also reduce racial and income segregation in housing patterns. Housing segregation is considered to be a major problem for a number of reasons: (1) it imposes a welfare loss on minorities by limiting and distorting their consumption of housing; (2) it contributes to the fiscal problems of central cities by concentrating the poverty problem within their borders; (3) it creates underfunded and segregated schools, which result in minorities obtaining inferior educations; and (4) it is contrary to the national policy goal of a fully integrated society. These, and still other reasons that could have been listed (see Kain and Persky 1969), provide a compelling case in favor of suburban dispersal of the minority population. The issue, however, is whether the dispersal proposal is practical.

Kain (1985) has argued that the suburbanization of the black population is possible and, contrary to the beliefs of many civil rights advocates and policymakers, it would not be required that suburban jurisdictions be forced to accept subsidized and other low-income housing. He used 1980 census data for Chicago to show that while blacks make up only 1.9 percent of all households living in suburban communities with above-average median income, they would have accounted for 14.8 percent of the households in these communities if household income had been the sole determinant of residential choice. He also shows that the central city share of SMSA black households in 1980 is 33.6 percentage points greater than would be expected from a knowledge of household incomes alone. This evidence, along with similar evidence provided by others (Taeuber and Taeuber 1965; Pascal 1967; Schnare 1977), provides strong support for the hypothesis that the exclusion of blacks from the suburbs can be primarily attributed to housing-market discrimination. Kain's policy recommendation is therefore to "strengthen enforcement of existing fair-housing laws and assist black households at all income levels to learn about and obtain housing in the nation's increasingly heterogeneous suburban areas."

The most serious criticism of the dispersal strategy is that of Muth (1985), who emphasizes that a clear distinction must be made between discrimination and prejudice as forces that determine segregated housing patterns. While it might be possible to open up the suburbs to blacks by the stronger enforcement of fair-housing laws, integration will not result as long as prejudiced whites react to the black infiltration by moving elsewhere. This, of course, poses an empirical question that future research should seek to answer; namely, will whites respond as Muth has suggested, and at what level of black in-migration will the white exodus occur? Within central cities, white flight from neighborhoods undergoing racial transition has been an important historical phenomenon. These results may not carry over into a suburban setting, however, since the cost of moving from the city to the suburbs may be quite different from the cost of moving from one suburban location to a more distant suburban location. At some point, the desire for access to the core may work to impede the mobility of white households.

There has been one experiment involving suburban dispersal: the Gautreaux Program. Begun in 1976, this program has assisted over 3,800 low-income black families to move from public to private housing in the Chicago metropolitan area. All of the families were originally central city residents and received Section 8 federal housing subsidies at their new location. Roughly half of the families were placed in suburban apartments located in predominantly white higher income neighborhoods. The other half remained within the central city.

Rosenbaum and Popkin (1990) have analyzed the postmove labor market experiences of female heads of households. Their results indicated that suburban movers are 14 percent more likely to have a job postmove than central city movers, after controlling for the respondent's work history, human capital, and personal characteristics. These results arc of interest, because they lend support to the spatial mismatch hypothesis and point to suburban dispersal as an effective means of improving job accessibility. The number of families participating in the Gautreaux Program, however, is too small to investigate Muth's concern regarding white flight; hence, the results of Rosenbaum and Popkin may not be generalizable to a full-scale dispersal of the minority population.

Ghetto development policies include providing subsidies to stimulate the growth of minority-owned business enterprises (i.e., black capitalism) and providing various financial inducements to attract firms to locate in the ghetto. As Bates and Bradford (1979) have shown, the experiences with black capitalism have not been encouraging. In recent years, the development proposal that has received the most attention has been the urban enterprise zone. As originally conceived, the zone would encompass an economically distressed area within the central city where taxes and government rules and regulations would be reduced or eliminated in order to stimulate the origination of small, new enterprises.

Federal legislation was originally proposed in 1980. This proposal, as well as many subsequent proposals, has failed to make it through the legislative process. Working against the passage of enterprise zone bills have been concerns over the costs and probable effectiveness of these areas. The critics have made three arguments:

1. The benefits accruing to individual firms from locating within an urban enterprise zone are insufficient to overcome the many other obstacles associated with a central city location, namely, crime, inadequate space, and higher wages for skilled employees.
2. Growth in jobs may occur as the result of zone inducements, but it will not result from the origination of new firms. Instead, growth will occur from existing firms or new firms—that would have started up even without the zone—choosing to locate in the enterprise area; hence, the zone's employment gain is offset by a loss in jobs somewhere else.
3. Regardless of the source of the job growth that occurs within enterprise zones, the expansion in jobs will not help indigent zone residents, because they do not possess the necessary skills for employers to hire them.

While the empirical evidence is not conclusive, it tends to contradict the notion that job growth will not occur within enterprise zones, but supports the arguments that jobs will come at the expense of other areas and will not go to zone residents. The evidence comes from studies of British enterprise zones (Schwarz and Volgy 1988) and zones established by state governments in the United States (Papke 1990; U.S. General Accounting Office 1988). The fact that most of the local gain in employment comes from the diversion of activity that would otherwise have occurred elsewhere is not necessarily bad. As this book has stressed, minorities and whites do not enjoy equal access to jobs. Reshuffling jobs from suburban to central city areas may be justified on a fairness criterion. In addition, the effects of the job loss experienced outside the enterprise area must be measured against the decline in crime and other antisocial behaviors committed by zone residents as the result of their improved employment opportunities. Finally, as Bartik (1991) has pointed out, individuals living in high unemployment areas probably place a higher value on getting a job than individuals in low unemployment areas; hence, the relocation of jobs in favor of zones may increase net social welfare.

The finding that most of the new jobs in urban enterprise zones do not go to zone residents is problematic. The policy implication is that zonal benefits should be made conditional on hiring the targeted population; however, this will reduce the incentive of firms to locate in the zone, since these workers will require more training. The significance of this problem has not been measured. But some people believe [see, for example, Heilbrun (1987)] that the attractiveness of enterprise zones will be seriously diminished under a commitment to hire the hardcore unemployed and to pay them a competitive wage.

Job creation programs involving subsidized temporary employment in the public or private sectors could be targeted specifically to central city minority youths. Fortunately, we have some knowledge of the probable effectiveness of such programs from the demonstration projects carried out under the aforementioned Youth Demonstration Act of 1977 (Betsey et al. 1985). The findings indicate that job creation programs are an effective means of raising the employment of both out-of-school and in-school teenagers. In fact, the previously described Youth Incentive Projects entitlement program succeeded in eliminating employment and unemployment differences between blacks and whites who were eligible for the program. The jobs provided by the Incentive Projects and the other Demonstration Act programs were, for the most part, minimum-wage jobs. The finding that program eligibles were willing to take these jobs is contrary to the hypothesis that the employment problems of minority youths are a function of their high reservation wage. The results from the Youth Demonstration Act projects are consistent with those presented in this study, in that both sets of results suggest that a significant part of the black youth employment problem is the unavailability of employment opportunities. Another finding from the Demonstration Act projects that has policy relevance is that the jobs provided to youths by various programs were generally not found to be of the make-work variety, but rather produced output that had value to the employer and to society in general.

Despite the above optimistic findings, there exists insufficient evidence to conclude that the benefits of temporary jobs programs exceeds their costs. For example, Youth Demonstration Act findings failed to provide reliable evidence on postprogram effects as well as on displacement effects, which should obviously enter into any calculations of benefits and costs. These are important areas for future research. Another more practical concern is that regardless of the outcome of cost-benefit studies, the significant cost of jobs programs may make them infeasible in light of present day budget realities.

References

Bartik, Timothy J. 1991. *Who Benefits from State and Local Development Policies?* Kalamazoo, MI: W.E. Upjohn Institute for Employment Research.

Bates, Timothy, and William Bradford. 1979. *Financing Black Economic Development*, New York: Academic Press.

Beasley, David. 1990. "Cobb Buses Take City Workers to Jobs." *The Atlanta Journal and Constitution*, 14 March, sec. A, p. 1.

Becker, Brian, and Stephen Hills. 1980. "Teenage Unemployment: Some Evidence of the Long Run Effect on Wages." *Journal of Human Resources* 15:197–211.

Becker, Gary S. 1971. *The Economics of Discrimination.* 2nd ed. Chicago: University of Chicago Press.

Bell, D. 1974. "Residential Location, Economic Performance, and Public Employment." In *Patterns of Racial Discrimination.* Vol. 1, edited by G. Von Furstenberg, A. Horowitz, and B. Harrison, 55–76. Lexington, MA: D.C. Heath.

Betsey, Charles L., Robinson G. Hollister, Jr., and Mary R. Papageorgiou. 1985. *Youth Employment and Training Programs: The YEDPA Years.* Washington, D.C.: National Academy Press.

Blinder, Alan. 1973. "Wage Discrimination: Reduced Form and Structural Estimates." *Journal of Human Resources* 8:436–455.

Borjas, George. 1986. "The Demographic Determinants of the Demand for Black Labor." In *The Black Youth Employment Crisis*, edited by R. B. Freeman and H. J. Holzer, 191–232. Chicago: University of Chicago Press.

Brownstein, V. 1989. "A Growing Shortage of Workers is Raising Inflation Risks." *Fortune*, 10 April, pp. 33–34.

Cogan, John F. 1982. "The Decline in Black Teenage Employment: 1950–1970." *American Economic Review* 72:621–38.

D'Amico, Ronald. 1984. "Does Employment During High School Impair Academic Progress." *Sociology of Education* 57:152–164.

Danziger, Sheldon, and Michael Weinstein. 1976. "Employment Location and Wage Rates of Poverty-Area Residents." *Journal of Urban Economics* 3:127–145.

Davidson, Charles. 1989. "Mass Transit Could Help, But Won't Solve Dilemma of Suburban Job Market." *Gwinnett Daily News*, 18 June, sec. D, p. 1.

Downs, A. 1973. *Opening Up the Suburbs*. New Haven, CT: Yale University Press.

Duncan, Beverly. 1965. "Dropouts and the Unemployed." *Journal of Political Economy* 73:121–134.

Edwards, Linda Nasif. 1976. "The Economics of Schooling Decisions: Teenage Enrollment Rates." *Journal of Human Resources* 10: 155–173.

Ehrenberg, Ronald G., and Alan J. Marcus. 1982. "Minimum Wages and Teenagers' Enrollment-Employment Outcomes: A Multinomial Logit Model." *Journal of Human Resources* 17:39–58.

Ekstrom, Ruth B., Margaret E. Goertz, Judith M. Pollack, and Donald A. Rock. 1986. "Who Drops Out of High School? Findings from a National Study." *Teachers College Research* 87:356–373.

Ellwood, David T. 1982. "Teenage Unemployment: Permanent Scars of Temporary Blemishes." In *The Youth Labor Market Problem: Its Nature, Causes, and Consequences*, edited by Richard B. Freeman and David A. Wise, 349–385. Chicago: University of Chicago Press.

———. 1986. "The Spatial Mismatch Hypothesis: Are There Teenage Jobs Missing in the Ghetto?" In *The Black Youth Employment Crisis*, edited by Richard B. Freeman and Harry J. Holzer, 147–187. Chicago: University of Chicago Press.

Farkas, George, D. Alton Smith, and Ernst W. Stromsdorfer. 1983. "The Youth Entitlement Demonstration: Subsidized Employment with a Schooling Requirement." *Journal of Human Resources* 4:557–573.

Farley, John E. 1987. "Disproportionate Black and Hispanic Unemployment in U.S. Metropolitan Areas." *American Journal of Economics and Sociology* 46:129–150.

Feldstein, Martin, and David T. Ellwood. 1982. "Teenage Unemployment: What Is the Problem?" In *The Youth Labor Market Problem: Its Nature, Causes, and Consequences*, edited by Richard B. Freeman and David A. Wise, 17–34. Chicago: University of Chicago Press.

Foderaro, Lisa W. 1990. "City to Suburb: Commuting Turns Around." *New York Times*, 10 January, sec. B, p. 1.

Franklin, James, B. McCummings, and E. Tynan, with contributions by E. Crowe and D. Landes. 1983. "Discrimination, Segregation and Minority Housing Conditions in Sunbelt Cities: A Study of Denver, Houston and Phoenix." Center for Public-Private Sector Corporation, University of Colorado, Denver. March.

Freeman, Richard B. 1982. "Economic Determinants of Geographic and Individual Variation in the Labor Market Position of Young Persons." In *The Youth Labor Market Problem: Its Nature, Causes, and Consequences*, edited by Richard B. Freeman and David A. Wise, 115–154. Chicago: University of Chicago Press.

———. 1991. "Employment and Earnings of Disadvantaged Young Men in a Labor Shortage Economy." In *The Urban Underclass*, edited by Christopher Jencks and Paul Peterson, 103–121. Washington, D.C.: Brookings Institution.

Freeman, Richard B., and David A. Wise. 1982. "The Youth Labor Market Problem: Its Nature, Causes, and Consequences." In *The Youth Labor Market Problem: Its Nature, Causes, and Consequences*, edited by Richard B. Freeman and David A. Wise, 1–16. Chicago: University of Chicago Press.

Freeman, Richard B., and Harry J. Holzer. 1986. "The Black Youth Employment Crisis: Summary of Findings." In *The Black Youth Employment Crisis*, edited by R. B. Freeman and H. J. Holzer, 3–20. Chicago: University of Chicago Press.

Friedlander, Stanley. 1972. *Unemployment in the Urban Core*. New York: Praeger.

Galster, George. 1987. "Residential Segregation and Interracial Economic Disparities: A Simultaneous Equations Approach." *Journal of Urban Economics* 21:21–44.

Gordon, Peter, Ajay Kumar, and Harry W. Richardson. 1989. "The Spatial Mismatch Hypothesis: Some New Evidence." *Urban Studies* 26:315–326.

Grant, James H., and Daniel S. Hamermesh. 1981. "Labor Market Competition Among Youths, White Women and Others." *Review of Economics and Statistics* 63:354–60.

Greene, Jane. 1981. *A Study of Housing Discrimination Against Mexican-Americans by Dallas Apartment Rental Agents*. November. Greater Dallas Housing Opportunity Center, Dallas, TX.

Greene, M.S., and B. Carton. 1986. "Jobs Program Places 2,271." *Washington Post*, 22 July, sec. A, p. 11.

Greytak, David. 1974. "The Journey to Work: Racial Differentials and City Size." *Traffic Quarterly* 28:241–256.

Gustman, Alan L., and Thomas L. Steinmeier. 1981. "The Impact of Wages and Unemployment on Youth Enrollment and Labor Supply." *Review of Economics and Statistics* 63:533–60.

Hakken, Jan. 1979. *Discrimination Against Chicanos in the Dallas Rental Housing Market: An Experimental Extension of the Housing Market Practices Survey*. HUD-PD&R-469, August. Office of Policy Development and Research, U.S. Department of Housing and Urban Development, Washington, D.C.

Harrison, Bennett. 1972. "The Intrametropolitan Distribution of Minority Economic Welfare." *Journal of Regional Science* 12:23–43.

Hausman, Jerry, and Daniel McFadden. 1984. "Specification Tests for the Multinomial Logit Model." *Econometrica* 52:1219–1240.

Heilbrun, James. 1987. *Urban Economics and Public Policy*. New York: St. Martin's Press.

Hill, C. R. 1979. "Capacities, Opportunities, and Educational Investments: The Case of the High School Dropout." *Review of Economics and Statistics* 61:9–20.

Holzer, Harry J. 1986. "Black Youth Nonemployment: Duration and Job Search." In *The Black Youth Employment Crisis*, edited by Richard B.

Freeman and Harry J. Holzer, 23–70. Chicago: University of Chicago Press.

———. 1987. "Informal Job Search and Black Youth Unemployment." *American Economic Review* 77:446–52.

Hughes, Mark Alan. 1987. "Moving Up and Moving Out: Confusing Ends and Means About Ghetto Dispersal." *Urban Studies* 24: 503–517.

———. 1989a. *Poverty in Cities*. Washington, D.C.: National League of Cities.

———. 1989b. *Fighting Poverty in Cities: Transportation Programs as Bridges to Opportunity*. Washington, D.C.: National League of Cities.

———. 1990. "Formation of the Impacted Ghetto: Evidence from Large Metropolitan Areas, 1970–1980." *Urban Geography* 11: 265–284.

Hughes, Mark Alan, and J. F. Madden. 1991. "Residential Segregation and the Economic Status of Black Workers: New Evidence for an Old Debate." *Journal of Urban Economics* 29:28–49.

Hutchinson, Lawrence. 1984. *Effects of Schooling on Cognitive, Attitudinal, and Behavioral Outcomes*. Columbus, OH: Ohio State University.

Hutchinson, Peter M. 1974. "The Effects of Accessibility and Segregation on the Employment of the Urban Poor." in *Patterns of Racial Discrimination*, edited by George M. von Furstenberg, Bennett Harrison, and Ann R. Horowitz, 77–96. Lexington, MA: D.C. Heath.

———. 1978. "Transportation, Segregation, and Labor Force Participation of the Urban Poor." *Growth and Change* 9:31–37.

Ihlanfeldt, Keith R. 1988. "Intra-Metropolitan Variation in Earnings and Labor Market Discrimination." *Southern Economic Journal* 55:123–40.

———. "Intra-urban Wage Gradients: Evidence by Race, Gender, Occupational Class, and Sector." *Journal of Urban Economics*. Forthcoming.

Ihlanfeldt, Keith R., and David L. Sjoquist. 1989. "The Impact of Job Decentralization on the Economic Welfare of Central City Blacks." *Journal of Urban Economics* 26:110–130.

———. 1990. "Job Accessibility and Racial Differences in Youth Employment Rates." *American Economic Review* 80:267–276.

———. 1991a. "The Effect of Job Access on Black and White Youth Employment: A Cross-Sectional Analysis. *Urban Studies* 28:255–265.

———. 1991b. "The Role of Space in Determining the Occupations of Black and White Workers." *Regional Science and Urban Economics* 21:295–315.

Jencks, Christopher, and Susan E. Mayer. 1990a. "Residential Segregation, Job Proximity, and Black Job Opportunities." In *Inner-City Poverty in the United States*, edited by Lawrence E. Lynn, Jr. and Micheal M. McGreary, 187–222. Washington, D.C.: National Academic Press.

———. 1990b. "The Social Consequences of Growing Up in a Poor Neighborhood: A Review." In *Inner-City Poverty in the United States*, edited by Lawrence E. Lynn, Jr. and Michael M. McGreary, 111–127. Washington, D.C.: National Academic Press.

Kain, John F. 1968. "Housing Segregation, Negro Employment, and Metropolitan Decentralization." *The Quarterly Journal of Economics* 82:175–197.

———. 1974. "Housing Segregation, Black Employment, and Metropolitan Decentralization: A Retrospective View." In *Patterns of Racial Discrimination*, edited by George M. von Furstenberg, Bennett Harrison and Ann R. Horowitz, 5–20. Lexington, MA: D.C. Heath.

———. 1985. "Black Suburbanization in the Eighties: A New Beginning or a False Hope?" In *American Domestic Priorities: An Economic Appraisal*, edited by John M. Quigley and Daniel L. Rubinfeld, 253–282. Berkeley: University of California Press.

Kain, John F., and Joseph J. Persky. 1969. "Alternatives to the Gilded Ghetto." *The Public Interest* 14:77–91.

Kalachek, Edward D., and John M. Goering. 1970. "Transportation and

Central City Unemployment." Institute for Urban and Regional Studies, Washington University, St. Louis, MO.

Kasarda, John D. 1989. "Urban Industrial Transition and the Underclass." *Annals, AAPSS* 501:26–47.

Leonard Jonathan S. 1986a. "Comments on: The Spatial Mismatch Hypothesis: Are There Teenage Jobs Missing in the Ghetto." In *The Black Youth Employment Crisis*, edited by Richard B. Freeman and Harry J. Holzer, 185–190. Chicago: University of Chicago Press.

———. 1986b. "Space, Time and Unemployment: Los Angeles 1980." Unpublished manuscript.

———. 1987. "The Interaction of Residential Segregation and Employment Discrimination." *Journal of Urban Economics* 21:323–46.

Lerman, Robert I. 1972. "Some Determinants of Youth School Activity." *Journal of Human Resources* 7:366–383.

McCosh, John. 1990. "Businesses Counting on Mass Transit to Boost Labor Pool." *Atlanta Journal and Constitution*, 5 November, sec. J, p. 1.

McFadden, Daniel. 1974. "The Measurement of Urban Travel Demand." *Journal of Public Economics* 3:303–328.

Margo, Robert A., and T. Aldrich Finegan. 1991. "The Decline in Black Teenager Labor Force Participation in the South, 1900–1970: The Role of Schooling." Working Paper no. 3704, National Bureau of Economic Research. (May).

Masters, Stanley H. 1974. "A Note on John Kain's Housing Segregation, Negro Employment, and Metropolitan Decentralization." *The Quarterly Journal of Economics* 88:505–519.

———. 1975. *Black-White Income Differentials: Empirical Studies and Policy Implications*. New York: Academic Press.

Mead, Lawrence M. 1987. "The Obligation to Work and the Availability of Jobs: A Dialogue Between Lawrence M. Mead and William Julius Wilson." *Focus* 10:11–19.

Meyer, R. H., and D. A. Wise. 1982. "High School Preparation and Early Labor Force Experience." In *The Youth Labor Market Problem: Its Nature, Causes, and Consequences*, edited by R. B. Freeman, and D. A. Wise, 277–339. Chicago: University of Chicago Press.

Mooney, Joseph D. 1969. "Housing Segregation, Negro Employment, and Metropolitan Decentralization: An Alternative Perspective." *The Quarterly Journal of Economics* May:299–311.

Morgan, William R. 1984. "The High School Dropout in an Overeducated Society." Center for Human Resource Research, Ohio State University. Mimeo.

Moulton, Brent R. 1990. "An Illustration of a Pitfall in Estimating the Effects of Aggregate Variables on Micro Units." *The Review of Economics and Statistics* 72:334–338.

Moulton, Brent R., and William C. Randolph. 1989. "Alternative Tests of the Error Components Model." *Econometrica* 57:685–693.

Muth, Richard. 1985. "Commentary." In *American Domestic Priorities*, edited by J.M. Quigley and D.L. Rubinfeld, 297–303. Berkeley, CA: University of California Press.

National Commission on Excellence in Education. 1983. *A Nation at Risk: The Imperative for Educational Reform*. Washington, D.C.: U.S. Government Printing Office.

Oaxaca, R. 1973. "Male-Female Wage Differentials in Urban Labor Markets." *International Economic Review* 14:693–709.

Offner, Paul, and Daniel H. Saks. 1971. "A Note on John Kain's Housing Segregation, Negro Employment, and Metropolitan Decentralization." *The Quarterly Journal of Economics* 191:147–160.

Orfield, Gary. 1985. "Ghettoization and Its Alternatives." in *The New Urban Reality*, edited by Paul E. Peterson, 161–196. Washington, D.C.: The Brookings Institution.

Osterman, Paul. 1978. "Race Differentials in Male Youth Unemployment." In U.S. Department of Labor, *Conference Report on Youth Unemployment: Its Measurement and Meaning*. Washington, D.C.: U.S. Government Printing Office.

———. 1980. *Getting Started: The Youth Labor Market*. Cambridge, MA: MIT Press.

Papke, James A. 1990. "The Role of Market Based Public Policy in Economic Development and Urban Revitalization: A Retrospective

Analysis and Appraisal of the Indiana Enterprise Zone Program." Year Three Report prepared for the Enterprise Zone Board, Indiana Department of Commerce, August 31.

Pascal, Anthony H. 1967. *The Economics of Housing Segregation.* Santa Monica: RAND Corporation.

Peirce, N.R. 1988. "Can the Suburban Jobs Boom Reach the Ghetto?" *National Journal*, 13 August, p. 2108.

Price, Richard and Edwin Mills. 1985. "Race and Residence in Earnings Determination." *Journal of Urban Economics* 17:1–18.

Reid, Clifford E. 1985. "The Effect of Residential Location on the Wages of Black Women and White Women." *Journal of Urban Economics* 18:350–63.

Roberts, Sam. 1990. "Migrant Labor: The McShuttle to the Suburbs." *New York Times*, 14 June, sec. B, p. 1.

Rose, Harold. 1972. "The All-Black Town: Suburban Prototype or Rural Slum?" In *People and Politics in Urban Society*, edited by Harlan Hahn. Beverly Hills: Sage Publications.

Rosenbaum, James E., and Susan J. Popkin. 1990. "Why Don't Welfare Mothers Get Jobs? A Test of the Culture of Poverty and Spatial Mismatch Hypothesis." Center for Urban Affairs and Policy Research, Northwestern University, Chicago.

Rumberger, Russel W. 1983. "Dropping Out of High School: The Influence of Race, Sex, and Family Background." *American Educational Research Journal* 20:199–220.

Schnare, Ann B. 1977. "Residential Segregation by Race in U.S. Metropolitan Areas: An Analysis Across Cities and Over Time." Contract Report no. 246–2. Washington, D.C.: Urban Institute.

Schwarz, John E. and Thomas J. Volgy. 1988. "Experiments in Employment — A British Cure." *Harvard Business Review*, March-April, pp. 104–112.

Stevenson, Wayne. 1978. "The Relationship Between Early Work Experience and Future Employability." In *The Lingering Crisis of Youth Employment*, edited by Arvil Adams and Garth Mangum, 93–124. Kalamazoo, MI: W.E. Upjohn Institute.

Stoker, Thomas M. 1986. "Consistent Estimation of Scaled Coefficients." *Econometrics* 54:1461–81.

Straszheim, Mahlon R. 1980. "Discrimination and the Spatial Characteristics of the Urban Labor Market for Black Workers." *Journal of Urban Economics* 7:119–140.

Taeuber, Karl E. 1983. "Racial Residential Segregation, 28 Cities, 1970–1980." Working Paper 83-12. Center for Demography and Ecology, University of Wisconsin, Madison.

Taeuber, Karl E., and Alma F. Taeuber. 1965. *Negroes in Cities: Residential Segregation and Neighborhood Change*. Chicago: Aldine.

Turner, Margery Austin, Michael Fix and Raymond J. Strayk. 1991b. *Opportunities Denied, Opportunities Diminished: Racial Discrimination in Hiring*. Washington, D.C.: Urban Institute Press.

Turner, Margery Austin, Raymond J. Strayk, and John Yinger. 1991a. *Housing Discrimination Study*. Washington, D.C.: U.S. Department of Housing and Urban Development.

U.S. Bureau of the Census. 1983a. Census of Population and Housing: Public-Use Microdata Sample (A and B Sample), (machine-readable data file), Bureau of the Census. Washington, D.C.

U.S. Bureau of the Census. 1983b. Public-Use Microdata Sample Technical Documentation. Prepared by the Data User Services Division, Bureau of the Census. Washington, D.C.

U.S. Bureau of the Census. 1984. 1980 Census of Population: Detailed Population Characteristics, U.S. Summary. Washington, D.C.: Bureau of the Census.

U.S. General Accounting Office. 1988. "Enterprise Zones: Lessons from the Maryland Experience." Washington, D.C., December.

Viscusi, W. Kip. 1986. "Market Incentives for Criminal Behavior." In *The Black Youth Employment Crisis*, edited by Richard B. Freeman and Harry J. Holzer, 301–352. Chicago: University of Chicago Press.

Vrooman, John, and Stuart Greenfield. 1980. "Are Blacks Making It in the Suburbs? Some New Evidence on Intrametropolitan Spatial Segmentation." *Journal of Urban Economics* 7:155–167.

White, Michelle J. 1976. "Firm Suburbanization and Urban Subcenters." *Journal of Urban Economics* 3:232–243.

———. 1978. "Job Suburbanization, Zoning and the Welfare of Urban Minority Groups. *Journal of Urban Economics* 5:219–240.

———. 1988. "Locational Choice and Commuting Behavior in Cities with Decentralized Employment. *Journal of Urban Economics* 24: 129–152.

Wilson, William Julius. 1987. *The Truly Disadvantaged: The Inner City, the Underclass and Public Policy* Chicago: University of Chicago Press.

Yinger, John. 1979. "Prejudice and Discrimination in the Urban Housing Market. In *Current Issues in Urban Economics*, edited by Peter Mieskowski and Mahlon Straszheim, 430–468. Baltimore: Johns Hopkins University Press.

Zax, Jeffrey S., and John F. Kain. 1991. "Commutes, Quits, and Moves." *Journal of Urban Economics* 29:153–165.

INDEX